Life, Death, and Public Policy

Life,
Death,
and Public Policy

Robert H. Blank

NORTHERN ILLINOIS UNIVERSITY PRESS

DeKalb, Illinois   1988

Library of Congress Cataloging-in-Publication Data

Blank, Robert H.
 Life, death, and public policy / Robert H. Blank.
 p. cm.
 Bibliography: p.
 Includes index.
 ISBN 0-87580-142-0
 ISBN 0-87580-540-X (pbk.)
 1. Medical policy—United States. 2. Medical technology—
Government policy—United States. 3. Medical technology—Moral
and ethical aspects. 4. Medical innovations—Evaluation. I. Title.
RA395.A3B544 1988   88-12453
362.1'0973—dc19   CIP

Design by Julia Fauci

To Charles O. Linnemeier

Contents

Preface

This book presents an overview of the hard life-and-death decisions that, increasingly, are making their way into the public-policy agenda. It describes the policy context of a broad array of biomedical innovations and analyzes the policy problems these advances are creating. Biomedical technology promises many benefits for many people, but it also raises critical dilemmas: when should they be used? who has the responsibility to decide? and who pays? As even more revolutionary technologies emerge, these issues become more complex.

No attempt is made here to provide an in-depth analysis of any single biomedical technology, nor does this book explore in any detail the ethical debate surrounding biomedical decisions. Instead, it focuses on the broader social-policy dimensions raised by this biomedical revolution in which even the basic definitions of life and death are challenged. Although selected technologies are described in order to illustrate the kinds of policy issues now emerging, technical details are minimized so that the book can be understood by informed citizens and students of the social and health sciences. References to more technical literature on each subject allow the reader to pursue any interests they may have for more extensive coverage of the techniques.

This volume also serves to introduce the Studies in Biomedical Policy series recently launched by the Northern Illinois University Press. Future offerings in this series will focus on specific biomedical applications and the policy issues surrounding them.

Many individuals deserve acknowledgment for their help in producing this book. Mary Lincoln of the NIU Press encouraged me to write this book and to edit the series on biomedical policy. The manuscript was strengthened considerably by Gary B. Ellis and Keith J. Mueller's valuable substantive comments and by Bruce Barron's excellent editing. I would also like to thank Karen L. Kapusinski, Carolyn Cradduck, and Christine Davidson of the Program for Biosocial Research at NIU for their work in transforming my handwritten scrawl into a readable manuscript. All these individuals have contributed to a stronger final product. Any remaining errors are my responsibility and should not reflect on any of these persons.

I want to also thank my wife, Mallory, and my children, Jeremy, Mai-Ling, and Maigin for their cooperation and patience. They have apparently survived yet another book.

Life, Death, and Public Policy

1 The Policy Context of Biomedicine

Aresident injects a terminal patient with a fatal dose of morphine. A surrogate mother and the couple who contracted with her to have a baby for them for ten thousand dollars go to court to win custody of the baby. A severely ill baby is kept in an intensive care unit for a year. Although the prognosis for the baby's long-term quality of life is low and the costs of her care already exceed one million dollars, the parents refuse to give up hope. A chronic alcoholic with cirrhosis of the liver goes to court to obtain public funding for a liver transplant while the parents of a six-month-old daughter appeal to the public for money to pay for a bone marrow transplant that will save her life. Although each case is unique, together they illustrate the broad range of issues emerging out of rapid advances in biomedical technology.

The rapid emergence of a broad assortment of biomedical technologies, represents a new revolution in modern society. Amazing advances in human genetic intervention (eugenics, sex selection, genetic counseling, genetic screening), reproductive technology (abortion, sterilization, prenatal diagnosis, artificial insemination, in vitro fertilization, fetal research), and biomedical intervention in the human life process (psychosurgery, electrical brain stimulation, drug therapy, and organ transplants) are challenging traditional values and social structures at an accelerating rate.

These issues present a formidable set of policy concerns that vividly demonstrate the critical ethical questions technological applications often raise.

Although the biomedical technologies now available pale in comparison to what is projected for the future, they already offer an impressive array of forms of intervention in human life. The ability to maintain life indefinitely by artificial means, new methods of creating and controlling life, and new applications of behavior control are likely to reshape our society in radical ways. Although these innovations offer new hope for many persons, they create previously unknown ethical and political dilemmas. New technologies have always demanded redefinition of issues and policies, but these modern discoveries and applications in genetics and medicine represent perhaps the greatest challenge our species has yet faced—the alteration of our most basic definitions of humanhood.

All biomedical technologies focus fundamentally on the question of the extent to which we ought to intervene directly in the human condition. They differ only with regard to the stage of human development with which a particular intervention is concerned (e.g., at conception, after birth, or at the end of life) and in the means of accomplishing the intervention, which range from legal restrictions on marriage for genetic reasons to sophisticated biomedical procedures such as gene surgery. Although each innovation offers it own opportunities and problems, these methods all share broader social and political ramifications which must be evaluated in a systematic and timely fashion.

This book addresses the issue of biomedical policy making within the context of accelerating advances in biomedical technology. As Figure 1 illustrates, the framework of biomedical policy is a complex one. In order to understand why particular policies are adopted, we must understand the demographic context, political and social values, and the medical structure as well as the technologies themselves. Policy responses to biomedical technologies also are shaped by public demands and expectations, the mass media, an array of concerned interest groups, and the structure of the political/legal system itself. Before examining in following chapters the specific technologies and the policy issues they raise, we must consider in greater detail this framework for studying biomedical policy.

Only major alterations in the U.S. health care system can avert a crisis of immense proportions in the coming decades. Many seemingly unrelated

Framework of Biomedical Policy

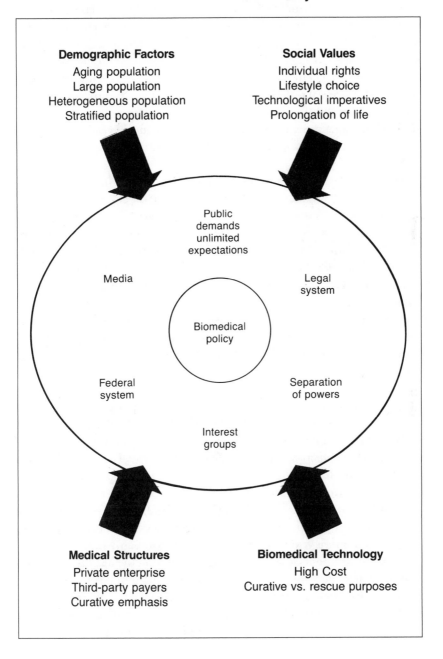

Demographic Factors
Aging population
Large population
Heterogeneous population
Stratified population

Social Values
Individual rights
Lifestyle choice
Technological imperatives
Prolongation of life

Public
demands
unlimited
expectations

Media

Legal
system

Biomedical
policy

Federal
system

Separation
of powers

Interest
groups

Medical Structures
Private enterprise
Third-party payers
Curative emphasis

Biomedical Technology
High Cost
Curative vs. rescue purposes

demographic, social, and technological trends promise to accentuate traditional dilemmas in medical policy making. The mushrooming elderly population; the proliferation of high-cost biomedical technologies designed primarily to extend life; the inadequacy of conventional retroactive reimbursement schemes by third-party payers to deal with these huge bills; and the general realization that health-care costs are outstripping society's perceived ability to pay—all lead to pressures for expanded public action. At the same time, public institutions appear unable and unwilling to make the difficult decisions in an area traditionally considered outside the political arena.

The confluence of these trends is certain to compound the already apparent constraints on economic resources. Despite all the current measures designed to contain costs, U.S. health-care expenditures are expected to increase from $387 billion in 1984 to $690 billion in 1990 and $1.9 trillion by 2000, representing almost 15 percent of the country's Gross National Product (Blendon, 1986:67). Moreover, health-care costs in the United States already average over $1,500 annually per person, compared to $450 in Great Britain.

Distribution of medical resources is heavily skewed toward a very small proportion of the population, further complicating the ethical dilemmas. More and more resources have been concentrated on a relatively small number of patients (most notably, the well-known transplant and artificial-heart cases) in acute care settings. For instance, intensive- and coronary-care cases alone account for approximately 15 percent of all hospital costs (Institute of Medicine, 1979:20). Similarly, in 1982, patients with end-stage renal disease, who represent less than 0.25 percent of all Medicare part B beneficiaries, accounted for over 9 percent of the total Medicare part B expenditures (Evans, 1983:2209). And overall, in 1975, 55 percent of all hospital expenses were incurred by only 4 percent of the patient population, or less than 1 percent of the entire population. The tough questions surrounding the just distribution of scarce resources in a society, therefore, become even more vexing in the establishment of biomedical priorities.

Increased competition for scarce resources within the health-care sector will necessitate decisions on allocation and rationing of resources (Blank, 1988). In turn, these actions are bound to exacerbate the social, ethical, and legal issues and intensify political action by affected individuals and groups. Although public officials may continue to sidestep making critical decisions and attempt to resolve long-term problems with piecemeal solutions, they cannot avoid becoming major participants in the health-care debate.

Biomedical Ethics and Public Policy

Until very recently, medical decision making has been a matter of private, not public, policy. Even the emerging emphasis on "bioethics" in the last several decades, while leading health-care facilities to include the ethical dimension in medical decision making through Institutional Review Boards (IRBs), did not immediately place these decisions in the public sector. The introduction of ethical considerations and their perceived escalation in importance did, however, contribute to the expanded role of public officials in medical policy making by requiring some form of protection of the interest of the weaker parties. Some agent was needed to ensure that these ethical concerns were properly considered before action was taken. Increasingly, public officials found themselves drawn into medical decision making in order to guarantee that ethical concerns were honored and the consumers of medicine protected. Tradition to the contrary, medicine was quickly drawn into the realm of public policy.

Although the emergence of interest in biomedical ethics and in biomedical policy are intertwined, the emphasis in policy analysis differs critically from that in bioethics. Health-care issues entail three crucial levels of policy decisions.

First, decisions must be made concerning the research and development of the technologies. Because a substantial proportion of medical research is supported, either directly or indirectly, with public funds, it is logical that public input be required at this stage. The growing, although still limited, interest in forecasting and assessing the social as well as technical consequences of health-care technologies early in research and development represents one attempt to facilitate a broader public input.

The second policy level relates to the individual use of technologies once they are available. Although direct government intrusion in individual health-care decisions is seldom warranted, the government does have at its disposal an array of more or less implicit devices to encourage or discourage individual use. These include tax incentives, provision of free services, education programs, and (perhaps most radical and controversial) rationing of health-care resources. Whether rationing will be a feasible future policy option remains to be seen. However, some observers feel that as the social costs of certain forms of treatment increase, we must begin to view physicians not simply as agents of the patients but also as trustees of scarce medical resources (Knaus, 1986).

The third, and perhaps most critical, level of health-care policy centers on the aggregate societal consequences of widespread application of a technology. For instance, what impact would wide diffusion of artificial heart transplants have on the provision of health care? Adequate policy making here requires a clear conception of national goals, extensive data to predict the consequences of each possible course of action, accurate means of monitoring these consequences, and mechanisms to cope with the consequences if they prove undesirable. Moreover, the government has a responsibility to ensure quality-control standards and fair marketing of all medical applications. As they become widely available, technologies which allow for sex preselection, surrogate motherhood, reversible sterilization, and gene surgery, will have sweeping social effects—on the family, on demographic patterns, and on the structure and size of the population. Policy planners must take these potential pressures on basic social structures into account as they decide whether and how to regulate the availability of these technologies.

The need for integrated and clearly articulated policy objectives to deal with the expanding arsenal of high-cost technologies is clear, yet the complex cultural, social, and political context of medical decision making makes such objectives very hard to develop. In a pluralist society, many conceivably legitimate but contradictory goals exist, especially on issues as fundamental as those relating to human life and death. Moreover, because these issues are not easily amenable to compromise, reaching a rational balance among the competing goals is a formidable task.

At its foundation, much of the controversy surrounding the development and application of biomedical technologies centers on conflicting goals and values criteria. Competing goal orientations, which frame public policy to varying degrees, are seeking to maximize: (1) individual freedom and choice; (2) social or public good; (3) scientific and technological progress; (4) quality of life; (5) human dignity; (6) efficiency; (7) social stability; and (8) alternative concepts of justice themselves based of goals of equity, merit, or need. Reactions to specific innovations, as well as to science and technology in general, will vary depending on one's predominant social values.

As medical technology pursues previously uncharted directions, assessing the social benefits and costs of each potential application becomes crucial. The diminishing lead time between initial research of a technique and its widespread dissemination, along with the potential irreversibility of many applications, demands analysis of technology early in the research and development process. David Freeman (1974:29) warns that technologies must be assessed before "unwanted, unanticipated, and damaging" consequences inflict "intolerable amounts" of harm on mankind. He fears that by the time the negative consequences are discovered, technologies have often become "frozen" within technical and institutional patterns, making changes designed to correct and control these consequences extremely costly and difficult.

Expectations of unlimited availability of medical technology, both among consumers and providers, pose another barrier to the creation of effective biomedical policy. These expectations fuel unrealistic public demands which, in turn, are encouraged by many providers of health services, who have a large stake in the continued growth of the health care industry. The infusion of corporate medicine and for-profit hospitals into the health-care community raises the stakes still further.

All political decisions involve tradeoffs as goods and services are distributed across a population. No matter what allocation scheme is applied, some elements of society will benefit and others will be deprived. The philosophical debate has long centered on what criteria ought to be used to determine whether or not a particular policy is just or fair. Do we select those policies that maximize the good for the greatest number, help those who are least well off, or concentrate on serving a small elite on the assumption that somehow benefits might "trickle down" to those on the bottom? Ever since Plato argued that health resources should not be wasted on the sickly and unproductive, the distribution of these limited resources has been a matter of public concern. But the dominant policy in the United States has been to minimize direct governmental intervention in the allocation of health-care resources. This policy perspective must be revised.

Until now, U.S. policy makers have tended to avoid making the difficult decisions regarding the distribution of scarce medical resources.

Most often their "solutions" merely shift costs from the individual to the government, or from one agency to another. Aaron and Schwartz (1984), for instance, perceive a pattern toward reliance on reimbursement of patient costs by insurance companies or government as a means of solving health-cost problems. Although this approach gives the appearance of resolving the problem, it only puts off the hard choices until later. William Brandon (1982) argues that we are running out of easy options and purported panaceas. The prevailing approach offers only interim shifts in the burden of payment and fails to address the critical issues of establishing policy priorities and setting limits on the use of certain high-cost medical technologies. Neither policy makers nor the public is willing to face the futility of simply shifting costs and to make difficult but increasingly urgent choices.

The Culture and Politics of Biomedicine in the United States

Observers of American society since Alexis de Tocqueville have commented on the uniqueness and internal diversity of values among its citizens. As a society, we emphasize individual autonomy, self-determination, personal privacy, and a shared belief in justice for all humans. Individuals in a liberal society are free to determine their preferred lifestyle for themselves and then, as long as they do not harm others, to live it. This general consensus of support for abstract values, entails the corollary that on issues of public concern, each person's views should be heard and all interests should be represented. The result is a proliferation of competing interests. Despite this diversity in viewpoints, though, the attempt to establish a biomedical policy interacts with several cultural themes that enjoy near-consensual support.

First, the prevailing value system places heavy emphasis on the notion of rights. Although the U.S. Constitution makes no mention of a right to health care, the courts often have interpreted the right to life to include an inherent claim of all citizens to health care and to autonomy in making decisions concerning health. In conflicts between individual rights and the common good or societal welfare, the individuals' claims to health care generally have taken precedence. Disputes continue, though, regarding the scope of individual rights, the extent to which society ought to intervene in these freedoms, and how such constraints, if any, might be justified. What responsibility does society have to protect a self-abusive individual? Ought the concept of community be expanded to take into account the rights of and our responsibilities toward the unborn, toward future generations, or even toward other species?

A second American value shaping decisions on health expenditures is the obsession with prolongation of life. Franz Ingelfinger (1980:143), swimming against this current, argues that too much money is spent to "convert Western octogenarians to nonagenarians." Saving an elderly person from one illness, often at great cost, only delays the inevitable and might very well expose that person to an even more debilitating disease. Although the quality of life of many aging persons is low and extensive technological intervention might prolong life only briefly, American society is excessively concerned with staying alive at all costs. Although there is considerable evidence that this mentality is changing, there remains a hesitancy to withhold any treatment, no matter how costly, which extends life. And by far the most expensive year of life for most persons is their terminal year.

Along with its significant emphasis, in the liberal tradition, on individual autonomy and a broad range of rights, American culture is also predisposed toward progress through technological means. Alexander Capron (1975:123) suggests that this value extends to medical technology through a deep commitment to the belief that medicine's progress will give us even greater powers over disease. This heavy dependence on technology to "fix" our health problems, at the exclusion of nontechnological solutions or prevention, is also tied to an American tendency to look always for the easiest solution. In the words of David Mechanic: "As a culture, we do far better in the application of a 'technological fix' than in building complex social arrangements that must be sustained over time in coping with expressive, frustrating, and often intractible problems" (1986:207). Americans use the benefits of technology in order to avoid more difficult changes in lifestyle. Should we encourage this perspective and develop technologies to provide a fix for problems like obesity, smoking, and sedentary life, or should we make efforts to alter our lifestyles?

Reiser (1985:171) cautions that technology can be addictive and compelling because it takes on a life of its own. We build into machines our aspirations and needs, he says. Like humans, once created, technologies seem to acquire a right to survive, to exist, and to make their mark. Because they have powerful symbolic meaning, medical devices such as the artificial heart are difficult to limit once they are introduced. Reiser (1985:173) argues that the technological fix approach is "generally wrong" because it does not adequately account for these complex effects of technology.

Reinforcing the public demand for increased development of medical technologies is the third-party reimbursement system, which by socializing risk and spreading out the costs, insulates much of the public from the real costs of meeting its high expectations. Instead of moderating expectations, the public demands more front-end insurance coverage to pay for high-cost medical care. As a society, we have come to expect the best science can offer when it comes to medical care for ourselves and our loved ones. We may complain about the high cost, but when our health or life is at stake we expect no expense to be spared. The preferred solution for many consumers is simply to shift the basis of payment to the government or private third-party payers. This ambivalence prevents any permanent solution to the problems of health-care costs. According to Brandon (1982:949), the result is a vicious circle. Rising health costs, combined with heightened public expectations, force people to obtain adequate medical insurance. However, the availability of more comprehensive insurance encourages overuse of medical care, thus driving prices up and making even more insurance necessary. The demand for expensive medical diagnostic and therapeutic technologies only accelerates this pattern.

It is not the public, however, who creates the initial demand for more advanced technology. Rather, the initiative for medical research and development comes from the scientists themselves. For instance, artificial-heart development was never demanded by the public, or even by an interested segment of it, but was stimulated by medical researchers (Office of Health Economics, 1979). These scientists create new needs that can be fulfilled only if new resources are made available. Because most health care is routine and not newsworthy, the media naturally focus attention on innovative techniques which can be easily dramatized. This media attention then leads to increased demand for the new procedure by both physicians and patients. Once the innovation passes the experimental stage, the consumers assume that it will become available for their benefit.

This process often oversells medical innovation and overestimates the capacities of new medical technologies for resolving health problems. Frequently the media report these innovations as medical "breakthroughs."

According to Ingelfinger (1980), organized medicine must share the blame for the overselling of medicine because it has encouraged society's belief in the omniscience of the medical profession. Also, physicians generally follow the technological imperative, which holds that a technology should be used if it offers any possibility of benefit, whatever its cost. Whether to protect themselves from malpractice suits, to provide the most thorough care for the patient, or to increase profit, many physicians would rather err—heavily—on the side of overusing diagnostic and therapeutic technologies. Ingelfinger also targets politicians who promise too much and attacks voluntary health groups that suggest in their fund-raising campaigns that if only more money were thrown into the research mill, major diseases could be contained.

The politically sensitive and controversial nature of these technologies, along with recent trends in the political arena and increased public awareness, demonstrates that technical decisions will no longer be made independently of politics. The 1970s saw a growing public role in biomedical research. Hanft (1977:19) views this emergence of public debate as resulting from inflation, multiplying health-care costs, and the general freedom-of-information climate. As the costs of research and application increase, public debate over priorities will expand. Because a large proportion of the funding comes from public monies, decision makers will scrutinize biomedical expenditures closely, producing an even greater dependence on the public sector.

A major factor contributing to the confusion and fueling the controversy over government involvement in biomedical technology is the inability or unwillingness to define clearly what such involvement could entail. Many observers emphasize the dangers of the form of state control they most fear while ignoring distinctions among the various types of governmental action. In actuality, governmental response to biomedical issues can take any one of four types or combinations thereof, including prohibition, regulation, encouragement, or mandate. Moreover, government intervention can occur at any point from the earliest stages of research to the application of specific techniques.

Some have proposed that the government actively outlaw certain types of genetic research and application. The 1974 Massachusetts moratorium on fetal research is an example of this form of social control, as are current attempts to prohibit reproductive research where human embryos are destroyed. Although many have called for the imposition of governmental prohibitions on biomedical research, most recently in the area of genetic engineering, it seems unlikely that the government will ban permanently specific areas of technology in the near future.

A second, more likely government option is the regulation of biomedical technology. Safety regulations, research priorities, and proper procedures, until recently viewed as matters for self-regulation by the scientific community, are increasingly coming under the purview of a variety of public institutions. Despite scientists' claims that such action results in cumbersome and unnecessary bureaucratic impediments to research, regulation will probably increase as these technologies become more available and opposition groups mobilize.

In contrast to controlling technology, government could also encourage development and application of biomedical technologies through use of discretionary measures intended to facilitate research and/or application of specific technologies. Because continued federal funding is crucial to the expansion of biomedical research, the government could through increased funding make current technologies available to all citizens who want to use it. Tax credits for medical expenditures or other incentive programs could also be implemented to encourage public use.

A final form of governmental action, most feared by those opposed to various human interventions, is the establishment of compulsory screening or eugenic (i.e., health-protecting) policies, on public-health or economic grounds. The compulsory sickle-cell screening legislation enacted in some states in the 1970s and compulsory PKU (phenylketonunia, a genetic disease causing mental retardation) testing programs are examples of such public intervention. Eugenic sterilization laws still on the books in some states represent a direct intervention in procreation. Other actions, such as recent efforts to require all applicants for marriage licenses to be tested for the AIDS virus, indicate that legislation of public-health measures is attractive to many segments of our society.

Few people fully understand the varied implications of each of these types of action. Those opposing government intervention as "intrusion" usually address only government prohibition or mandated eugenic policy. Those supporting government involvement usually refer to the more moderate forms of control represented by regulation and encouragement.

Another factor contributing to the confusion over governmental intervention is the failure to distinguish between the technologies themselves and the uses to which they are put. Often the debate becomes garbled because the participants fail to clarify that they are in fact discussing particular uses of the technology rather than the techniques. Persons opposing biomedical technologies often focus on potential coercive uses (involuntary sterilization, compulsory genetic screening, active euthanasia) or political abuses (human experimentation, psychosurgery, eugenics programs) of specific techniques, whereas those who support them deal exclusively with clinically indicated applications and minimize the possibility of coercive applications. Greater conceptual clarity would narrow (though not eliminate) the controversy over biomedical technologies.

American Political Institutions and Biomedical Policy

An understanding of the political structures, institutions, and processes that define the boundaries of policy making is essential in order to comprehend the particular priorities and the apparent inconsistencies found in the health-care system. In the United States, this political context includes the basic institutions of federalism, separation of powers, and popular consent as well as the actual procedures of policy making. Increasing attention on the part of several branches of government has not yet rescued biomedical policy from a morass of fragmented, uncoordinated, and often contradictory actions taken by a myriad of agencies and committees.

Congress

The federal legislative process as now constituted is not designed to handle the kind of issues raised by biomedical technology. As a deliberative body, Congress is extremely slow both in recognizing policy problems and in acting upon them. According to Shick (1977:10), the "legislative process is weighted against quick and comprehensive responses" and encourages bargaining and compromise to build majorities at each stage. The issues raised by biomedical technology, however, are qualitatively different from traditional public issues revolving around expenditures of funds. Although biomedical issues include that dimension, they also pose difficult ethical and moral questions, which political institutions prefer to avoid. Reliance on current political procedures results in failure to recognize the richness and complexity of these issues. As Coates (1978:33) asserts, "cut and fit accommodation and incremental change, the traditional strategies of government, are increasingly ineffective, if not sterile modes of operation." Moreover, Congress's committee system increases duplication of efforts on cross-cutting issues as numerous committees stake claims to jurisdiction, further slowing the process without assuring that relevant policy interdependencies will be considered. Because biomedical issues combine what in the past were perceived as separate issues and multiply the number of interests that must be considered, the process is further frustrated.

It should be noted that state legislatures, which retain considerable jurisdiction on public health do no better. In addition to sharing the above problems, they usually have inadequate staff and resources to familiarize them with these issues. Furthermore, the presence of fifty separate legislative frameworks leads to unsystematic and often inconsistent policy on these sensitive issues.

In the 1985 Health Research Extension Act, Congress attempted to address these concerns by creating a Biomedical Ethics Board, composed of six senators and six representatives, with an equal number of members from each party. After more than a year of foot-dragging and in-fighting, in August 1987 the Board finally appointed its advisory committee of experts in the fields of law, medicine, and ethics (Gianelli, 1987:10). This fourteen-member committee was mandated by the 1985 act to counsel members of Congress on the ethical issues arising in the delivery of health care and in biomedical research. The battle over selection of members focused mainly on their views on abortion and other life-related issues. The Board's proposed role in biomedical policy is off to a less than impressive start.

Most legislators are hesitant to become embroiled in these issues. Especially if (as in the case of the U.S. House of Representatives) they are up for reelection at frequent intervals, they try to avoid controversial issues that might trigger single-issue group action against them. The political issues raised by biomedicine, therefore, seldom generate significant enthusiasm or activity until the situation becomes desperate enough to require action. Even then, the response takes the form of patchwork disaster control rather than long-range, definitive policy.

Barring widespread public demand for a comprehensive revision of health-care policy, Congress is unlikely to undertake it. Rather, Congress will meet the demands of powerful interest groups through piecemeal legislation, which is often inconsistent and counterproductive. While the health-care establishment cannot achieve all its goals, in part because of the lack of a consensus among its many components, it has been largely successful in keeping change to a minimum. Since the general public is silent or tolerant of the status quo, the most salient pressure on congressmen comes from groups opposed to restructuring of health care. In this situation, the lack of vigorous, future-oriented deliberation on these issues by public officials who desire reelection should not be surprising.

The Bureaucracy

The size and complexity of the federal bureaucracy, combined with a splintered distribution of jurisdictional boundaries, results in overlapping lines of authority. Given the historical development of the various agencies and the competitiveness of these agencies for power and influence, there is nothing approaching a single locus of power for biomedical policy making. No coordinating mechanism exists to ensure that policy is consistent or to eliminate the duplication and confusion that ensue when more than one agency makes policy in the same general area. Nor do these agencies always cooperate fully with each other—thereby further preventing production of a comprehensive, foresighted policy.

Another problem inherent in bureaucracies, which minimizes their objectivity and causes them to lose sight of broader public responsibilities, is their dependence on the support of special-interest groups. If the government is to make objective and comprehensive biomedical policy, it must create an agency relatively free from dominance by interest groups yet open to widespread public access. This event seems unlikely within the current institutional context, where the growth and survival of a public agency depends on its success in establishing routinized relationships with its clients. The bureaucracy, at least as it now operates, appears incapable of dealing with the complex and controversial problems raised by biomedical technologies.

Several recent developments appear to signal a move toward more active government involvement in biomedical issues. Within the Department of Health and Human Services (HHS), the Office of Health Technology Assessment was established to coordinate analysis and testing by agencies; to determine safety, efficacy, and cost effectiveness of new and existing biomedical technologies; and to assist in determining which mechanisms should be used to promote, inhibit, or control the use of these technologies. Also within HHS, the National Institutes of Health (NIH) created an Office for the Medical Applications of Technology.

The Courts

In large part because of the inability of other branches of government to address the issues raised by biomedical innovations, the courts currently play a central role in policy making. Unlike legislatures, the courts cannot shirk their agenda; they must make decisions on the cases brought before them. Also, because the issues raised by medical technology center on questions of individual privacy and autonomy, due process of law, and conflicts over rights—all issues traditionally resolved by the courts—it is natural that the judicial branch be at the forefront of biomedical policy.

Despite the continuing debate over whether courts ought to make public policy and a growing concern over their capacity to make decisions based on medical or biological fact (Blank, 1986), the courts are heavily involved in all facets of biomedicine. From abortion to surrogate mother-hood to organ transplants to pulling the plug, the courts daily make decisions that produce a common-law policy context. Moreover, the courts' heavy involvement in medicine via malpractice suits has tremendous influence on the practice of medicine by defining professional standards of care and encouraging the technological imperative.

At this stage the courts are unmistakably involved in deciding appropriate uses of health-care technologies. According to May (1981:120), state courts are pressing deeper into the medical community, taking away its authority to make decisions free from outside control. Courts are heavily involved in governing the delivery and quality of medical services through their action on statutes that set policies, create control agencies, and generally influence medical practice, as well as through medical malpractice lawsuits. May (1981:122) contends that the courts' rejection of the locality rule, by which physicians were held to local standards rather than more stringent national ones, has led to greater patient rights and higher expectations of health-care delivery. Ironically, this shift has also broadened the court deference to expert testimony from the national medical community at the expense of the individual physician and forced the courts to become embroiled in an increasingly complex, professionalized, and expert-dominated set of policy issues.

Can judges secure and understand the medical "facts" needed to resolve these highly complex questions? Although the problems involved in the courts' entrance into cases requiring substantial technical knowledge has received little systematic analysis so far, there is growing concern over the capacity of judges to respond to scientific testimony and to make decisions on scientific fact (Rist and Anson, 1977). There are also broader questions as to how well the courts use scientific terms and concepts in reaching their conclusions.

In his detailed critique of the courts' involvement in social policy making, Horowitz (1977:31) concludes that judges not only lack information themselves but may also lack the experience and skill necessary to interpret such information if they receive it. Judges are generalists, not specialists. One consequence of the "generalist dominance" in the courts according to Horowitz (1977:25) is that in the "interstices where expertise is lacking, the generalist fills the gaps with his own 'generalized normative axioms.'" Lack of attention to specialized facts is, therefore, a characteristic of the judicial process. Critics such as Horowitz call for either enhancement of judicial capacity to handle scientific data and to foresee the consequences of court action, or greater judicial hesitancy in making policy in those substantive fields where their capacity is most limited.

Matheny and Williams (1981:349) add that the adversarial system, in which both sides present evidence they claim favor their position, itself works against adequate use of biological fact and proper resolution of technically complex disputes. Some means must be devised to ensure that scientific testimony is properly used. Even so, the evidence is not always conclusive, and the courts must be prepared to pass judgment in such cases because these problems are critical and demand resolution. For Rosen (1972:11), "A basic problem for the Supreme Court is not whether it will allow fact situations to influence its interpretation of the Constitution, but whether it will in adjudicating any given issue accept a statement of the relevant facts prepared by a lower court or, instead, set forth its own understanding of the facts."

Other observers are less willing to acknowledge that the courts are incapable of integrating scientific data into their decisions. Youngblood and Folse, although agreeing with many of Horowitz's criticisms, note that court orders must be based on the Constitution and not on the theories of social scientists and others. They also (1981:30) dispute the contention that judges cannot deal with facts and argue that there is ample opportunity for specialists to contribute in the courts. In addition to the tremendous staff and research resources available to judges, the adversary process can help to give the judge relevant information. Amicus curiae briefs and substantive specialization in some courts mean that judges are not always scientific novices (Youngblood and Folse, 1981:30).

Whatever the capacity of courts to integrate facts, Youngblood and Folse contend that they should not attempt to balance the facts. Judges should make decisions on their "commonsense understanding of human nature" and their "sense of fairness operating within the confines of principle," not solely on the basis of the facts in a technical sense. Youngblood and Folse strongly reject Horowitz's alternatives of reformulating court techniques to handle facts or of avoiding policy making in technical fields. In their view, neither prescription is compatible with the traditional role of the courts and either course of action would ultimately threaten their legitimacy as governing bodies. "Were a court to approach its task by identifying and balancing the social costs and benefits of various outcomes, it would be doing something other than articulating or preserving rights . . . the court would no longer be operating within the confines of principle" (Youngblood and Folse, 1981:58). Judicial decisions, then, should not be based on assessment of the social costs and benefits of alternative outcomes even if the courts could determine them. These authors reject any attempts to alter judicial decision making to sharpen the focus on policy consequences.

Although the major transformations of the judicial process advanced by Horowitz may be an overreaction, critical adjustments in how courts deal with biological facts are essential. Primarily, judges must be more fully aware of the ramifications of their action when they use biological fact as part of their rationale for a ruling. The courts are put in a difficult position when they base decisions on biological rationale, especially when they fail to recognize or understand the extent to which technological advances are altering biological "fact." These controversies have an "inherently hybrid technical and legal character" and "present issues that can be resolved by neither purely technical nor purely legal analysis" (Yellin, 1981:491). These issues force the courts to deal not only with new forms of information but also with new methods of analysis of causality, methods which are totally alien to the language and mode of analysis of the legal profession. It is not surprising that these new demands on the courts are producing severe strain.

As the courts are drawn further into a broad array of biomedical areas, including organ transplantations, human genetic intervention, neonatal intensive care, and the allocation of scarce medical technologies, it is crucial that the judiciary, the legal profession, and students of public law become aware of the policy implications of these advances in medicine. These areas promise to offer some of the most difficult constitutional, contractual, and civil questions in the upcoming years. They relate directly to our basic conceptions of what it means to be human. All sensitive biomedical issues will be tested in the courts, and the most difficult ones will eventually make their way to the U.S. Supreme Court, which, isolated from public pressures, will make its highly controversial rulings.

Proliferation of Interest Groups

Interest groups concerned with biomedical issues, though recent in origin, have quickly expanded in number and scope. Because biomedical intervention enhances or threatens many individuals' strongly held values, interest-group activity surrounding these issues will continue to grow, especially in this period of heightened competition for scarce resources. Our pluralistic culture and political tradition encourage the creation of interest groups to advance the concerns of their members. The policy process guarantees that such groups will have a powerful influence on public policy.

Several interest groups have successfully influenced biomedical policy, through their lobbying efforts. To a large extent the National Sickle Cell Anemia Control Act (1972), the National Cooley's Anemia Control Act (1972), the Huntington's Chorea and Hemophilia Act (1975), and the various kidney dialysis statutes reflect the successful lobbying efforts of individuals and groups concerned with each particular disease. The more recent "Baby Doe" legislation (Child Abuse Amendments, 1985) was the direct result of lobbying by a coalition of right-to-life and handicapped advocacy groups. At the core of recent demands for governmental funding of heart and liver transplants are special-interest groups organized specifically for that purpose.

One of the more interesting developments in the debate over genetic and reproductive issues, in that it bridges traditional liberal-conservative political lines, is the new alliance evolving against these technologies. These issues have created cleavages among traditional allies and have linked unlikely groups together in their opposition to particular technologies. Until recently, conservative groups who reject reproductive intervention on moral grounds, most notably the "pro-life" coalition of Catholics and fundamentalist Protestants, have been the most salient opponents of biomedical technology. However, these rightists have been joined by liberal elements who fear repression, stigmatization, or invasion of privacy. Racial minority leaders have publicly criticized various biomedical technologies as contrary to the interests of their communities. Feminist leaders, too, have decried these innovations because they threaten the role of women in society. Finally, a liberal "concerned scientists" lobby has been organized by Jeremy Rifkin and others to stop or inhibit the proliferation of these technologies.

Interest-group activity in biomedical issues will continue to cut across traditional social and political cleavages in American society. Because of the complexity of the problems these technologies raise and the value conflicts they produce, future alignments of groups will differ substantially from those on other political issues. This makes it highly unlikely that either political party will be able to adopt a strong policy stand on biomedical issues without risking loss of substantial bases of support. At the same time, the high stakes involved in policy decisions concerning intervention in the human condition will accentuate group activity and magnify conflict among the interests.

The Mass Media and Biomedical Issues

These groups know the "power of the press" and are using the mass media effectively to publicize their concerns and provide the public with information about technological developments. Because the media finds biomedical "breakthroughs" so newsworthy, dramatic and widespread coverage is common. Front-page headlines on the first test tube baby, the surrogate-mother case of Baby M (*Stern v. Whitehead,* 1987), the artificial heart, and premature announcements of treatments for AIDS, all are quickly supplanted by reports on the next technological wonder. Such stories find a welcoming audience because they reinforce faith in the "technological fix."

In his critique of the 1970s debate over recombinant DNA in the mass media, Grobstein (1979:104) contends that the press itself is an important interest group that "finds grist for its own mill in emphasizing the more spectacular alternative scenarios and the clash of the more charismatic personalities." He asserts that in its own version of the public interest, the media exaggerates confrontation but ignores the duller details of the resolution of such conflicts. In spite of their inherent biases toward sensationalism and simplification of the issues, the media remains for most citizens the single source of information concerning these issues.

Urgent: *Policies Needed*

The rapid diffusion of biomedical technology, in conjunction with social and demographic trends, requires increasingly arduous decisions as to how to best use them. As we come to realize that we cannot afford to do everything for everybody, we are thrust into policy dilemmas that deal directly with human life and death. These dilemmas become all the more difficult as we continue to develop remarkable ways to intervene directly in the human condition, from before conception to life extension. Just when we have the technical capacity to do things we only recently even dreamed of, rising expectations and scarce resources combine to limit their availability. The resulting need to allocate biomedical technologies, in turn, raises critical concerns over whose needs take precedence, what individual rights and responsibilities arise, and when societal good justifies restrictions on individual good. These policy issues, although by no means new, take on a new importance within the context of emerging conflicts accentuated by our technological successes in biomedicine.

In an effort to make some semblance of order out of the myriad of biomedical technologies, I have grouped the technologies into four categories, each corresponding to intervention at a different life stage. Under this scheme, technological interventions are classified as occurring (1) at or prior to conception, (2) during the prenatal period, (3) within the life cycle, or (4) at the end of life. Although the issues across these stages are similar in nature, they differ in detail. The clarity these distinctions add to the discussion outweighs the dangers inherent in any categorization scheme of this type.

Chapter 2 examines the technologies and accompanying policy concerns involved in human genetic and reproductive intervention. For convenience, chapter 2 discusses the applications of genetic technology on adults, as well as those related to reproduction. Chapter 3 extends this analysis into the prenatal period and surveys the array of policy issues emerging from new diagnostic and therapeutical techniques available at that stage. Chapter 4 covers the period from birth through life and discusses issues such as intensive care, behavior modification, and organ transplantation. Chapter 5 looks at death-related issues in biomedicine, and chapter 6 returns the discussion to problems of allocation of medical resources with particular emphasis on the issues raised by AIDS. No pretense is made here as to the inclusiveness of the technologies discussed. Instead, I have tried to select a set of technologies in each chapter that elucidates the policy issues of biomedicine without overwhelming the reader with technical information.

2 Human Genetic and Reproductive Intervention

Until recently, humanity had no control over the genetic quality of the progeny it procreated. Infertile persons had little hope of solving their problem. Just a decade ago, the capacity to remove fertilization from the secrecy of the womb to the bright lights of the laboratory was, one might say, inconceivable. Today's brand-new remarkable genetic and reproductive interventions represent a veritable revolution. As such, they bring not only stunning change but also critical questions as to what implications that change has for individuals and society as a whole.

The rapid succession of advances in human genetics and the shortened lead time between basic research and application make genetic intervention especially controversial. Fundamental values tend to change slowly across generations. The success of genetic technology threatens these values, but allows little time for careful reflection. As a result, value conflicts arise rapidly and zoom inevitably into the public-policy arena.

In addition to challenging basic values, human genetics raises the specter of eugenics and social control for many. References to a *Brave New World* scenario, in which human reproduction is a sophisticated manufacturing process and a device for maintaining social stability, are commonplace, as are comparisons to Nazi Germany. Moreover, opponents of human genetic engineering—and "engineering" becomes a highly pejorative word in this context—describe the process as interfering with evolution or even playing God. Not surprisingly, in view of this characterization, opposition to genetic and reproductive intervention is frequently intense.

Another complicating factor which heightens opposition to genetic intervention among some groups is the selective nature of genetic diseases. The success of genetic-screening efforts often depends upon the ability to isolate those groups who are at high risk. Targeting these groups, however, raises problems of stigmatization, due process, and invasion of privacy. The early experience with sickle-cell screening, for instance, led to perceived and real threats to the black community and aroused severe criticisms of screening efforts. As DNA probes are used to identify individuals at heightened risk for alcoholism or personality disorders, the issue of stigmatization is bound to reemerge, thus making any attempts to screen extremely controversial.

Human Genetic Technology

The precursor issues in human genetic intervention have arisen from carrier-screening techniques. The primary clinical objective of screening for carrier status is to identify those individuals who, if mated with another person with that same particular (recessive) genetic trait, have a 25 percent chance that their offspring will have the disease. Once identified, parents with carrier status can be offered prenatal diagnosis if it is available for that disease or, they can be informed of the risk that they take in having children. Because the carriers do not have a disease, genetic screening of this type is indirect: it is not beneficial to the health of those screened but, rather, to potential persons who have a one-in-four chance of having the disease if they are conceived and born.

Carrier-screening programs have been in effect in many states and localities for Tay-Sachs disease and sickle-cell anemia for almost two decades. The sickle-cell programs have been especially controversial because the trait is concentrated in the black population. Carrier-screening tests for many recessive genetic diseases and even more precise genetic trait markings will be available in the near future. The most rapid developments have been in the area of DNA probes to identify genetic signs of a particular trait. Following the discovery of such a molecular probe for the Huntington's disease gene in 1983, efforts have been initiated to identify genetic markers for Alzheimer's disease (Kolata, 1986c), manic depression (Kolata, 1986a), malignant melanoma (Kolata, 1986d), and a host of other conditions. In addition, considerable attention is being directed to the genetic bases of alcoholism, and work is proceeding at a rapid pace toward development of techniques to identify persons susceptible to alcohol dependency. A major research initiative is underway to map the entire human genome—that is, to identify the placement of all the genes on all the chromosomes (Lewin, 1987). One particularly sensitive area of research seeks to discover which genes are associated with intelligence. Work on the "fragile-X" chromosome is the first wave of this inquiry (Partington, 1986). Eventually, genetic tests will allow scientists to identify not only the course of genetic abnormalities, but also traits that put certain individuals at higher risk for susceptibility to a host of environmental factors.

Ironically, these new capabilities will accentuate the political, legal, and ethical issues involved in genetic counseling and screening. When screening leads to prevention or treatment of genetic disease, the issues, though often controversial, are reasonably straightforward. However, when screening involves identifying heightened risk or susceptibility for particular conditions, it is considerably more problematic. And when it is based on controversial assumptions, such as the influence of heredity on intelligence, it is politically explosive. As new diagnostic tests and genetic probes emerge, public demand for accessibility to these controversial sources of genetic information will increase. Once the tests become accepted as legitimate by policy makers, it is likely that legislatures and courts will recognize professional standards of care that incorporate them. Recent legislation in California, requiring physicians to order alpha-fetoprotein tests for pregnant women, and similar court decisions involving a variety of prenatal tests illustrate the public-policy dimensions inherent in these applications.

Genetic screening has key implications not only for reproductive decisions but for the adults themselves, as more precise and inclusive tests enable us to identify people at high risk for a disease or condition. Increasingly, genetic counselors are facing pressures from employers and insurance companies for access to information obtained from these tests (Kolata, 1986b). This issue has been smoldering for several decades in conjunction with sickle-cell carrier screening and workplace screening (Hubbard and Henifin, 1985). Holden (1982:336) points out that although there are "probably thousands of genetic deficiencies that render individuals unusually vulnerable to certain chemicals," only a few presently are known. To date the most commonly screened traits have been the sickle-cell trait; glucose-6-phosphate dehydrogenase deficiency (G6PD), which can predispose carriers to a disintegration of red blood cells if exposed to certain chemicals, and alpha-1 antitrypsin (AAT) which can predispose individuals to lung disorders and emphysema from exposure to lung irritants.

Many employers feel they should know if an employee is at heightened risk for occupational hazards, and some companies have initiated their own genetic screening programs, amidst considerable controversy (Matthewman, 1984). Although usually defended on the grounds that it is for the employee's benefit, such action also reflects a fear of liability suits either by the employee or by others who might be harmed by that employee's actions. Potential capabilities raised by DNA probes to identify persons at risk for alcoholism, Alzheimer's disease, manic depression, and other conditions accentuate the issue. When, if ever, is the patient's right to privacy to be sacrificed for the interests of the employer? Under what circumstances does the genetic counselor's responsibility to society outweigh his or her responsibility to the patient? Increased knowledge about specific susceptibilities related to a wide variety of genetic traits and more accurate tests for these traits will only sharpen the debate. Harsanyi and Hutton (1981:248) expect the "art of prediction" of screening genetic markers "will be refined to the point where an individual's identification with various groups, along with the genes that he carries, will pinpoint the risks he faces from specific environmental conditions." They go on to contend (1981: 262) that, although the workplace should be made as safe as possible for all workers, those found to be at greatest risk should "either find another job or accept responsibility for the illness to which they are predisposed."

Insurance companies, too, have a substantial stake in data obtained through these methods. Life-insurance companies, which normally exclude from their programs people who are poor health risks, are keenly interested in the results of tests which identify those individuals at high risk for particular diseases. Likewise, health-insurance companies, especially now that they face new competition from alternative models such as health maintenance organizations (HMOs), will want access to test results, particularly if they are paying for the tests. Insurers know that a large proportion of health-care costs are attributable to a small proportion of their members, and they will be under severe economic pressure to use all tests available to identify individuals genetically predisposed to ill health or to conditions such as alcoholism and eliminate coverage for them, thus reducing overall costs substantially. As with employers, genetic counselors are bound to be at the center of these competing pressures for information on the results of genetic tests.

Although the courts have upheld the constitutionality of premarital tests in instances of communicable diseases, screening for genetic traits is more controversial. Given the current state of genetic technology, premarital screening would focus on testing the prospective husband and wife to determine whether they could transmit recessive diseases such as sickle-cell anemia, galactosemia, or Tay-Sachs disease. Such a program would be effective only if couples at risk altered their reproductive plans by either not procreating or by making full use of available prenatal diagnostic technologies. It is not clear how such a program would be enforced once the couple had been informed of their genetic status. There is considerable disagreement about the usefulness of mandatory premarital carrier screening (Blank, 1981:129). Among its proponents, however, is the Chicago Bar Association, which proposed in 1974 that all applicants for marriage licenses be tested for carrier status (Beckwith, 1976:53).

Human Gene Therapy

The next logical step beyond diagnosis of genetic disorders is gene therapy. Although extensive human gene therapy is not imminent, at least six major research centers in the United States are working to develop such techniques. These procedures would correct genetic defects, not by environmental manipulation, but instead by acting directly on the DNA in the affected person's cells. One approach, which has been tried on some victims of sickle-cell anemia and thalassemia (another genetically caused form of anemia), is to "turn on" certain genes which would otherwise be inactive, so that they can take over the job of the defective genes. Another possible approach would introduce normal genes into chromosomes of cells that contain defective genes in the hope that the manipulated cells would ultimately replace the defective ones, thus curing the patient.

The major research emphasis today is on somatic cell therapy, in which genes are inserted not into germ cells (that is, sperm, egg, and cells that give rise to sperm and egg) but into other body cells. Because somatic cell gene therapy does not affect the germline, the genes conveyed through the procedure would not appear in the recipient's progeny. Considerably more controversial than this replacement of a defective gene in somatic cells is the direct intervention in germline cells—those which contribute to the genetic heritage of offspring. "In this case, gene therapy has the potential to affect not only the individual undergoing the treatment but his or her progeny as well. Germline gene therapy would change the genetic pool of the entire human species, and future generations would have to live with that change, for better or worse" (Olson, 1986:50) Both technical difficulties and ethical concerns make it extremely unlikely that germline gene therapy will be attempted in the near future (Olson, 1986:50).

According to W. French Anderson of the National Heart, Lung, and Blood Institute, the first diseases selected for treatment by somatic cell gene therapy will share three important characteristics (1984:403). First, they will be diseases arising from a defect in a single gene which causes the loss of an enzyme and thus produces severe suffering or premature death. To date only a few of the more than two-hundred single genes known to cause human disorders have been isolated and reproduced through genetic engineering so that their copies can be inserted into cells.

Second, these diseases will be ones treatable through genetic manipulation of bone marrow cells, because techniques have been developed to remove these cells from the body, transform them with recombinant DNA, and reintroduce them into the body. Although it might be possible in the future to genetically manipulate skin cells or even tissues and whole organs, to date bone marrow cells are the only cells conducive to this kind of treatment (Olson, 1986:45). Finally, the genes responsible for the diseases must operate a fairly simple kind of regulation—preferably an "always-on" type. According to the National Institute of General Medical Sciences (1984:54), three major hurdles to gene therapy remain: learning how to *deliver* the normal gene to the proper target cell and having it stay there; getting the normal gene *expressed* by producing what it should and regulating it properly; and ensuring that the new gene does no harm.

This step from diagnostic to therapeutic ends of genetic intervention poses difficult questions regarding the role the government ought to play in encouraging or discouraging research and application. It also raises ethical questions concerning parental responsibilities to their children, society's perceptions of children, the distribution of social benefits, and our definition of what it means to be a human being.

Despite these concerns, there is a growing consensus among persons who have studied somatic gene therapy that it would be unethical to deny this treatment to desperately ill patients once the basic technical conditions of delivery, expression, and safety are satisfied (Olson, 1986:48). Under these conditions somatic cell gene therapy would differ little in its practical application from traditional treatments, particularly bone marrow and organ transplantation. The only significant difference is that this therapy operates at the gene level. Grobstein and Flower (1984:14), however, suggest that if reproductive health includes the probability of having genetically normal offspring, an individual needing gene therapy could claim an ethical right not to be deprived of direct germline repair since, without this more radical procedure, all the individual's offspring would at least be carriers of the gene: "Although somatic cell therapy might be provided in each generation, the argument to rid the lineage of the defective genes once and for all might prove compelling."

Sex Preselection Technologies

Interest in sex selection is certainly not new. Many cultures have long used infanticide in order to achieve this goal (Hughes, 1981). According to the government's Office of Technology Assessment (1981a:312), though, current Western interest in sex selection stems from animal research, initiated because predetermining the sex of the progeny of dairy cattle, for instance, could yield large financial benefits. Public demand has shortened considerably the usual lead time between animal and human application of these techniques. Although estimates vary as to when sex preselection will become widely available for humans, sex selection kits are already being marketed in the United States by Pro-Care Industries, Ltd. under the name Gender Choice.

The approaches that now appear to offer the best chances of success in human application are based on the fact that each sperm cell carries either an X chromosome or a Y chromosome and that the progeny's gender is determined by which type of sperm fertilizes the egg. The goal of sex preselection is to control which type of sperm fertilizes a particular egg. Some recently discovered characteristics of these two types of sperm help to make this objective possible. First, in any male ejaculation Y-bearing sperm are more numerous, smaller, and less dense and move faster than their X-bearing counterparts. Conversely, the Y-bearing sperm die sooner and are more readily slowed down by normal acidic secretions of the vagina. However, they are less inhibited than the X-bearing sperm by the alkaline environment of the uterus once they pass the vagina.

Within the context of this new knowledge about the sperm, most of the current research on sex preselection is seeking to develop accurate and reliable sperm separation techniques. Various sedimentation processes, centrifugation, and electromagnetic forces have been used. Once the desired sperm concentrations are isolated, they are inseminated into the recipient woman's uterus by artificial insemination.

Another possible means of separating the X- and Y-bearing sperm is to insert a special type of diaphragm in the woman's reproductive tract to screen out the larger X-bearing sperm and allow passage to the egg of Y-bearing (male) sperm only. Hartley and Pietraczyk (1979:234) point out, however, that because sperm are microscopic in size, designing such a membrane presents a yet unsolved technical difficulty. Other promising sex preselection techniques include the use of special foams or jellies developed to affect the motility of one or the other type of sperm, perhaps in combination with the special diaphragm or with prophylactics designed to screen out the X-bearing sperm.

Although we appear far from translating this technology into acceptable, simple, and usable methods of application, sex preselection is now within the grasp of human endeavor. Furthermore, the frantic research activity in other areas of genetic and reproductive intervention makes it clear control of human characteristics other than sex is on the horizon.

Policy Issues in Sex Preselection

As American couples today have fewer children than ever before, they are particularly interested in technologies that offer control over the characteristics of their progeny. Although preference for a particular gender is less clear in the United States than in many other cultures, the availability of sex preselection techniques combined with the trend toward one- and two-child families undoubtedly will produce a broad demand. Also, as sex selection techniques move from the highly intrusive to less intrusive methods, demand will increase. The establishment of for-profit sex selection services will develop to meet this demand, because it is unlikely that existing non-profit fertility clinics will be able to make a commitment to these methods that have no medical benefit except in those few instances where they could avert gender-related genetic diseases. Part of the controversy over the development and diffusion of sex-selection innovations centers on survey data suggesting that males would more often be selected, especially where couples desire only one child.

Although no simple, reliable, and usable method of sex preselection has received wide acceptance from the research community, demand for services is already accelerating as the media publishes fragmented reports of success. Unlike in vitro fertilization and other reproductive techniques, sex selection appears to have a large potential market. It is thus an area where an industry that markets sex-selection products and services could exploit couples' desires to control the gender of their progeny. It takes little imagination to picture the forms a sex-selection advertising campaign might take.

As of 1987 at least twenty clinics in the United States were using variations of the sperm separation procedure to select sex-specific sperm. Although most clinics are primarily experienced in choosing Y-bearing or male producing sperm, several are working with both sex chromosomes. In 1984 researchers at Swedish Hospital in Seattle claimed a 96 percent success rate in isolating X-bearing sperm by using a sperm sifting process. Their procedure utilizes a three-foot-long, pencil-thin glass column filled with a gel. The semen filters down through the gel and drains into a series of test tubes. Researchers then pick the three to five tubes with the cloudiest material and sample each, staining them with a yellow fluorescent dye and examining them by microscope under mercury vapor light. Male chromosomes show up with a bright yellow spot while female ones do not show up at all. The sperm sample with the highest concentration of X-bearing sperm is artificially inseminated into the woman desiring a female offspring.

Although Swedish Hospital inseminates the woman the same day as the sperm separation procedure is conducted, there is no biological reason why cryopreservation (freezing) could not be used to store the sperm sample for future insemination. When refined, techniques such as this one could be used in combination with AID (artificial insemination by donor sperm) or in vitro programs to maximize the chances of producing a child

of the desired sex. In addition to overcoming infertility problems, this procedure would also allow the couple an opportunity to select the sex of
their progeny with a high degree of accuracy. In a competitive market
setting, the demand for sex selection might force clinics to make it available, despite the ethical problems it raises concerning the manipulation of
the reproductive process.

Intervention in Human Reproduction

We are quickly entering the second phase of a revolution in human
reproduction which began with the separation of sexual intercourse from
reproduction through widespread use of the "pill" and other contraceptive
innovations in the 1960s. This second phase provides a corollary to the contraceptive revolution by separating reproduction from sexual intercourse—
giving us the means to reproduce without sex. It promises to bring with it
severe alterations in social attitudes and behavior that will exceed those
changes still reverberating from the first stage. The challenges raised by
this aggregation of reproductive technologies that alter the "givens" of
human reproduction raise critical public-policy issues which must be
addressed promptly. Artificial insemination, in vitro fertilization, embryo
transfer, cryopreservation techniques, and an array of imminent innovations allow for many combinations of human germ material outside conventional sexual reproduction. These technologies will have considerable
input on a variety of social structures.

Technologies of Human Reproduction

Infertility is a growing problem for many American men and women.
In 1982, an estimated one in six couples was infertile. The causes of infertility are complex and poorly understood but do include environmental,
inheritable, pathological, and sociobehavioral factors. Although drug
therapy and microsurgical intervention have effectively treated infertility
in some instances, couples are turning increasingly to reproductive technologies. According to the Office of Technology Assessment (1987a:1),
the demand for these services is enhanced by several factors:

1. Couples are delaying childbearing, thereby exposing themselves to
   the higher infertility rates associated with advancing age.

2. Increased awareness of the availability and success of modern infertility services has been coupled with a decreased supply of infants available for adoption. In 1983, about 50,000 adoptions took place in the United States, but an estimated 2 million couples wanted to adopt.

3. A greater number of physicians offer infertility services than in previous years. An estimated 45,600 physicians provide infertility services, exceeding by 25 percent the number of physicians providing obstetric care.

The most widely used form of reproduction-aiding technology today is artificial insemination (AI). It is estimated that approximately 500,000 children have been born in the United States to women fertilized by this method (most with donor sperm—AID). Between 30,000 and 60,000 AIs are being performed annually in the U.S., resulting in 6,000 to 12,000 births. Although it is the simplest of available techniques, AI still brings into the reproductive process third parties in the form of physicians or other interveners. Also, it introduces the concept of collaborative conception. Despite its relatively long history and high use, there are no consistent policy guidelines for AI across the states.

Although the first reported child conceived through AID was born a century ago, its use has expanded in the last few decades by the introduction of cryopreservation techniques which freeze and preserve sperm indefinitely by immersion in liquid nitrogen. Cryopreservation has led to the establishment of commercial sperm banks, some of which now advertise their products to the public. Sperm banks also make it possible for a man to store his semen prior to undergoing a vasectomy as a form of "fertility insurance." More importantly, they also facilitate eugenic programs, such as the Repository for Germinal Choice which inseminates women of "high intelligence" with sperm of "superior men" (Isaacs and Holt, 1987:13).

In vitro fertilization (IVF) is a procedure by which eggs are removed from a woman's ovaries, fertilized outside her body, and reimplanted in her uterus. This procedure is used when the oviducts are blocked, preventing the egg from passing through the fallopian tubes to be fertilized. Andrews (1984:123) estimates that 490,000 American women might be helped by this technique. The highly sensitive oviducts are easily scarred by pelvic inflammatory diseases or other low-level gynecological infections, thus blocking passage of the ovum to the sperm. Contemporary social patterns, including increased sexual contact of young women with a variety of partners, are also linked with increased infertility in women. The epidemic proportions of gonorrhea, and more recently, Herpes Simplex II, and Chlamydia (which also can lead to blocked oviducts) among young women promise to accentuate this problem.

In vitro fertilization expands considerably the possible combinations of germ material and further complicates the concept of parenthood. It has also gained rapid popularity. In 1978 the first in vitro baby, Louise Brown, was born in England. In January 1980, after considerable political debate, Norfolk General Hospital obtained governmental approval to make the technique available. On December 28, 1981, Elizabeth Carr became the first in vitro baby born in the United States. Within six years, the number of clinics offering IVF in the U.S. expanded to over 150, and the number of children born through this method has surpassed 3,000.

Moreover, most IVF clinics continue to have long waiting lists of women willing to pay $4,000 to $5,000 for a chance of becoming pregnant. In most cases, the final cost of pregnancy is over $25,000 because several attempts are necessary. Despite this investment, up to 80 percent of the women who undergo IVF do not become pregnant. Some couples have gone through the process up to eight times without success. Pressures are mounting on insurance companies to cover all or part of the procedure, and some are doing so. In October 1987, Massachusetts became the first state to adopt a statute that requires private insurance companies, but not Medicaid, to cover the costs of all treatment designed to overcome infertility, including IVF. If costs are reimbursed in whole or in part by third-party payers, demand will escalate even faster. Once the technologies become available and are proven effective, their diffusion across the country is guaranteed because the pool of candidates for technology-mediated procreation is a growing one.

This heavy demand for reproductive-aiding technologies led in 1983 to the first birth through the embryo lavage technique. In this particular case, twelve potential donor women were artificially inseminated with the sperm of the husband of a couple. After a sophisticated procedure in which the menstrual cycles of the donor women and the wife were synchronized, the embryos were flushed from the donors at about five days and microscopically screened. The best (based upon technical criteria of cell division) embryo was selected and transferred to the wife who carried it to term. Although the procedure was performed at Long Beach (California) Memorial Hospital, it was a Chicago firm, Fertility and Genetics Research, Inc., which applied for patents for both the procedure and the computer software.

Perhaps the most controversial social innovation culminating from these technological breakthroughs has been surrogate motherhood. In this arrangement an infertile woman and her husband contract with another woman (the surrogate), who agrees to be artificially inseminated with the husband's sperm. After fertilization, she carries the fetus to term; once the baby is born she relinquishes her rights to it and gives it to the couple. Surrogate motherhood raises new legal and moral problems because the surrogate must be willing to be inseminated by the sperm of a stranger, carry his baby for nine months, and then give the baby to the couple or the single man who contracted with her, usually for a fee. The surrogate mother makes a substantial commitment, both physically and emotionally. Moreover, the couple must rely on the surrogate to keep her promise because they cannot be assured of any legal rights to the child. The 1988 decision by the New Jersey Supreme Court *(Stern v. Whitehead),* which declared surrogate contracts invalid and in violation of State adoption laws because of the payment, may have a chilling effect should other states follow suit.

In addition to these already available techniques, still more revolutionary innovations are forthcoming. Egg fusion, or the combination of one mature egg with another, eliminates the need for male genetic material and always produces a female. In an extension of this technique, both eggs could be obtained from the same woman, thus producing a daughter who is totally hers genetically. Reproductive-aiding technologies also overlap with screening and selection technologies. Sperm separation techniques used in conjunction with AID and IVF can enable infertile couples not only to have a child but to choose its sex. Increasingly precise genetic diagnosis using molecular probes of embryos prior to transfer will make possible even greater control over the characteristics of our progeny.

All reproductive technologies share the ethically acute characteristic of introducing a third party into what has been a private matter between a man and a woman. The more complex the intervention, the more mediators are necessary. Embryologists, geneticists, and an array of other specialists become the new progenitors. Although these specialists' desire to help desperate patients may be genuine, their very presence takes control of procreation away from the couple. The willingness of many infertile couples to do (and pay) anything to have a child also encourages the commercialization of procreation. Heightened demand could lead to exploitation of the consumers of these services. As in all health care, a tiered system, in which the technologies serve primarily the upper middle class, may be developing.

Given the spread of fertility problems among American couples, the demand for these innovations will increase significantly. However, because of their perceived threat to conventional notions of parenthood, family, and procreative autonomy, these technologies are potentially explosive political issues.

Policy Issues in Reproductive Technology

At the very least, these rapid advances in reproductive technology force us to reevaluate our beliefs concerning reproduction and the right of procreation. In a broader sense, they challenge traditional notions of parenthood. Now we must learn to distinguish among the genetic parents (who contribute the germ material), the biological mother (who carries the fetus to term), and the legal parents, one or both of whom may also be the genetic parents. Moreover, the extent to which these artificial methods of reproduction involve considerably more individuals (often third parties with a commercial interest) than the natural method means procreation is a public matter. Depending upon their specific application, these technologies can be viewed as either extending or constraining procreative rights. Every reproductive technology is open to a variety of clinical and eugenic applications, depending upon the motivation of the persons using it.

Perceptions of Children.   Widespread use of the new array of human genetic and reproductive intervention technologies will have substantial long-term implications for society's perceptions of children. As couples (and singles) have fewer children, parents who envision having a "perfect child" increasingly seek the assistance of these technologies. Many young couples are going to considerable lengths to ensure the birth of a near-perfect child (Bishop and Waldholz, 1986). Survey data indicate that many parents would consider termination of a pregnancy even because of moderate defects in the unborn child such as a heightened risk of early heart disease or criminal tendencies. Parents have even sought growth hormone therapy for a young child simply because the child is not expected to reach the parents' desired height. The quest for the perfect child is becoming an obsession.

This emphasis on technological perfection raises questions concerning the purpose of having children and tends to commodify them. It is not surprising that discussions of "quality control" over the reproductive process or of children as "products" of particular techniques are commonplace. Motivations for the application of reproductive techniques must be examined closely, for the trend to view children as commodities poses a clear danger to the concept of personhood.

Furthermore, the availability of technologies for prenatal diagnosis, screening, and selection may heighten discrimination against children born with congenital or genetic disorders. In fact, it may be that acceptance of selective abortion is already reducing tolerance of those living with the unwanted conditions. Leon Kass (1976:317) expresses concern for those abnormals who are viewed as having escaped the "net of detection and abortion" as attitudes towards such individuals are "progressively eroded." In this atmosphere, increasingly such individuals will be seen as unfit to live, as second-class humans, or as unnecessary persons who would not have been born if only someone had gotten to them in time. Parents are likely to resent such a child, especially if social pressures and stigma are directed against them. The "right to be born healthy," say Murphy, Chase, and Rodriquez (1978:358), is misleading because it actually means that "only healthy persons have a right to be born." To Alexander Capron (1979:681), the recognition of an enforceable right to be born with a sound, normal mind and body would "open the door to judicially mediated genetic intervention of limitless dimensions." For many of those affected, the choice is not between a healthy and unhealthy existence, but rather between an unhealthy existence and none at all.

Reproductive Technologies and Reproductive Rights.   No issue in the last decades has been more heatedly debated in America than that of reproductive choice. The right to privacy in reproduction has been at the center of the women's movement for equal status in a society that has often denied them equality due to their prime role in reproduction. The progression of Supreme Court decisions on procreative privacy (beginning with *Skinner v. Oklahoma* (1942), continuing with *Griswold v. Connecticut* (1965) and *Eisenstadt v. Baird* (1972), culminating in *Roe v. Wade* (1973), and reiterated by *City of Akron v. Akron Center for Reproductive Health* (1983) has clearly enunciated a woman's constitutional right not to conceive or bear a child if she so desires—including access to contraception, sterilization, and abortion without state interference. Despite significant violation in practice, the conceptual right to reproductive privacy is well established.

Although abortion remains a volatile issue, the complementary issue of whether all women (and men) have a corresponding right to have children is just as problematic. Can any limits be imposed as to the number or quality of one's progeny? For instance, can carriers of genetic disease be prohibited from conceiving children from their own germ material and required to use collaborative-conception technologies such as AID or embryo transfer? Must a woman avail herself of prenatal diagnostic techniques to identify defective fetuses? Must she abort or permit in utero treatment of a defective fetus? Women have been ordered by courts to undergo cesarean sections against their wishes for the benefit of the fetus (Blank, 1986: 464ff). Should they, as a matter of public policy, also be required to permit invasion of their body for surgery on the fetus in utero? If so, who makes the policy and how is it implemented?

Until now, reproductive choice largely has been framed as a *negative* right, assuring only that the choice cannot be constrained without a "compelling state interest." In the absence of a state interest that overrides the individual's choice, she or he has a right to reproduce as long as the action does not harm a constitutionally defined person. The emergence of reproductive and genetic technologies, while it drastically extends the potential scope of procreative choice, also threatens the rights to reproduction privacy that women have gained in the last two decades.

Reproductive technologies raise the possibility of reproductive autonomy as a *positive* right—a claim upon society to guarantee, through whatever means available, the capacity to reproduce. If the right to procreation is interpreted as a positive one, then an infertile person might have a constitutional claim to these technologies. Under such circumstances, individuals unable to afford the treatments necessary to achieve reproductive capacity could demand society's help. A woman with blocked fallopian tubes would have a claim to corrective surgery or in vitro fertilization. An infertile man would be ensured access to artificial insemination or, if possible, corrective surgery. Once procreative rights are stated as positive, however, drawing reasonable boundaries becomes difficult. For example, could a woman who is unable to carry a fetus to term because of a high-risk condition or the absence of a uterus claim the right to a surrogate mother? Wherever the lines are drawn, some individuals will still find their opportunity to have children limited.

The advent of the new reproductive technologies raises serious questions regarding procreative choice. Any shifts toward a positive-rights perspective will accentuate the already growing demand for these technologies, encourage entrepreneurs to provide a broad variety of these reproductive services, and, most importantly, put increasing pressures on the government to fund these services.

Reproductive Responsibility: Ethics of Genetic Gambling.   In the last section we asked whether carriers of recessive genes and persons with dominant diseases have a duty to either refrain from procreating or utilize collaborative conception technologies, such as artificial insemination or embryo transfer, so that these deleterious genes are not transmitted to their offspring. Some contend that "it is wrong to reproduce when we know there is a high risk of transmitting a serious disease or defect" (Purdy, 1975:28).

With current techniques in artificial insemination, cryopreservation, and embryo transfer, these individuals no longer need refrain from conception in order to avoid having defective offspring. Now, for instance, if a husband is suspected of carrying a dominant gene for Huntington's Disease, he can use the services of a sperm bank. Although this process eliminates his biological contribution to the child, it also eliminates the 50 percent risk of the child having the disease. Similarly, if both persons in a couple are identified as carriers of a recessive disease they can: (1) take a 25 percent chance that a child born to them will have the disease; (2) undergo prenatal diagnosis, if available for that disease, and abort the fetus if it is identified as having the disease; or (3) use reproductive technology, such as artificial insemination, and be content with a healthy child, albeit one which is not genetically their own.

Although these options are currently open to couples, the key question is whether a couple has the responsibility to avoid option 1 and, thereby, the chance of bearing a child with a genetic disease. Does a child born with Tay-Sachs disease, which can be diagnosed prenatally, have grounds for action against a physician who fails to advise the use of artificial insemination? If the physician or genetic counselor recommends such action and the parents refuse, should the parents be liable for the wrongful life of their child? Ethical and legal guidelines have not kept pace with the availability of the technologies in this area.

Sterilization

Ironically, one of the most persistent social policy issues in human reproduction is the converse of the reproduction-aiding technologies, sterilization. Moreover, new technological developments in human sterilization promise to complicate rather than resolve the constellation of constitutional, political, and social problems surrounding the termination of fertility. Most prominent in this array of emerging techniques are reversible sterilization methods that are less intrusive than traditional surgical procedures.

The interest in reversible sterilization can be understood best by examining the convergence of several social and technical patterns. First, voluntary sterilization has become a popular method of birth control—after all, it is the only completely effective method. Studies of contraception practices demonstrate a clear and definite trend toward increased use of sterilization as birth control. A survey by Forrest and Henshaw (1983) found that American women who practice birth control rely more often on sterilizing themselves or their male partners than on any other method. The data suggest that 11.6 million couples depend on sterilization while some 9.9 million women use birth-control pills. Over 17 million persons in the U.S. have been sterilized; worldwide, sterilization is by far the single most used form of fertility control.

Long-term fertility control is as elusive now as it was two decades ago. Most couples still elect to have small families while they are young and are then faced with upwards of twenty years of fertility control. Rather than use a form of contraception which is at best inconvenient and not fully effective and is at worst a significant hazard to the woman's health, more couples are opting for sterilization as a permanent solution.

The extremely high rate of divorce and remarriage in modern America has stimulated increased demand for reversible methods. Individuals who were sterilized voluntarily and enthusiastically during their first marriage decide after remarrying that their sterilized state is unacceptable. Renewed interest in having children with their new partners often results in attempts to reverse sterilization. Also, a growing number of women who had been sterilized for career reasons are deciding later in life that they want children. Although most individuals choosing sterilization are reasonably certain they wish to terminate their fertility permanently, a growing number are demanding a form of safety net in case they change their mind.

Despite considerable strides in the technology for reversing "permanent" sterilization procedures, the Association for Voluntary Sterilization still considers it standard procedure to advise women seeking tubal sterilization and men undergoing vasectomy that these are permanent methods of fertility control which may be not reversible. Even when a highly trained surgeon uses the most refined instruments and newest techniques, the chances for reversal of tubal ligations and vasectomies are not high. In addition, some sterilization techniques destroy major sections of the reproductive anatomy and thus make reversal virtually impossible. Current research, therefore, is emphasizing techniques designed to be reversible from the start.

Reversible Sterilization Techniques

Of the many current research approaches, the one that may drastically revise concepts of sterilization and contraception is the removable silicone plug (RSP). This method involves the occlusion of the woman's fallopian tubes with flexible plugs. Unlike conventional sterilization procedures, RSPs are specifically designed to be removed at a later date so as to permit childbearing (Wimberley, 1982:1).

This procedure makes use of developments in fiber optics so that the physician can observe the installation of the silicone in the fallopian tubes. A hysteroscope is introduced through the cervix and into the uterine cavity. A liquid silicone mixture is pumped into the oviduct where it solidifies in approximately five minutes. A nylon retrieval loop placed in the silicone allows for later removal by grasping the loop with a forceps and literally "pulling the plug."

The RSP procedure involves less than one hour in an out-patient surgical facility, plus several follow-up sessions. Reversal is expected to be a relatively simple office procedure, although clinical testing so far has focused only on the implantation. Clinical trials conducted in the early 1980s demonstrated success rates of between 80 and 90 percent in occluding the fallopian tubes. Removable silicone plugs are currently being offered as a sterilization technique in many clinics, although the consent form to be signed by the patient usually describes it as a technique that *might* be reversible—no guarantees. Despite cautions that these questions of reversibility are yet unanswered (Wimberley, 1982), RSP shows great promise and thereby challenges currently held notions of sterilization as nearly always irreversible (Cooper and Houck, 1983:268). Initial successes will stimulate increased demand for reversible RSP services.

In addition to RSPs, various other approaches have been proposed to block the passage of the egg from the ovaries through the fallopian tube. Trials are now proceeding with many of these methods, including hug plastic clips, tubal hoods, Teflon plugs, and burying or attaching a prosthesis to the fimbrial (far) end of the fallopian tubes. Although theoretically these procedures may be more reversible, Henry, Rinehart, and Piotrow (1980:c107) note that "there is no information available to date either on reversals performed or on subsequent pregnancy rates."

Sterilization Policy and the New Technologies

When based on the patient's informed and voluntary consent, sterilization is an effective means of fertility control. But nonconsensual, or in some cases compulsory, sterilization raises policy questions of a basic constitutional nature. If the distinction between voluntary and nonconsensual sterilization were precise, the dilemma would be lessened considerably. Unfortunately, such precision is not possible, and most of the controversy over sterilization centers on situations where the question of free choice may not be clear.

In the United States, initial interest in sterilization was based on social control, not on the grounds of individual choice. Early legislation was motivated both by medical theories that claimed mental illness was inherited and by social elitist theories stemming from social Darwinism (Kevles, 1986). In 1907 Indiana passed a Eugenic Sterilization Law that sought to eliminate retardation simply by sterilizing relevant target groups of "unfit" individuals. Eventually thirty more states passed legislation that empowered mental and corrective institutions to sterilize inmates. In some states, such as Washington, statutes were extended to permit punitive sterilization of certain felons (especially those convicted of rape), chronic alcoholics, and derelicts.

The extent to which the eugenic logic dominated American society appears clearly in Justice Oliver Wendell Holmes' affirmation, in *Buck v. Bell* (1927), of the state's duty to impose sterilization as an appropriate exercise of its police power. Holmes's conclusion that "three generations of imbeciles are enough" is a cogent reminder of how faulty medical theory can affect even the Supreme Court. That decision's callous disregard for the rights of the individuals concerned was not questioned until *Skinner v. Oklahoma* (1942), in which the court ruled that a state law authorizing involuntary sterilization of particular felons violated their right to equal protection. According to Justice Douglas, marriage and procreation are civil rights of man, fundamental to the very existence and survival of the race: "The power to sterilize, if exercised, may have subtle, far-reaching and devastating effects. . . . There is no redemption for the individual whom the law touches. Any experiment which the state conducts is to his irreparable injury. He is forever deprived of a basic liberty." Although *Skinner* did not address directly the question of eugenic sterilization, it made procreative freedom a fundamental right which cannot be readily violated.

Although *Skinner* repaired the most glaring constitutional deficiencies, revised statutes permitting nonconsensual sterilization in limited cases have been upheld by a succession of courts. In most cases, these revisions reflect a noticeable shift in the rationale for sterilization from the largely discounted eugenic arguments to a concern for the best interests of the affected individuals or their potential progeny.

Three themes characterize the resurgence of proposed sterilization legislation since the 1970s. The first is the presumption that mentally retarded persons are incapable of being fit parents; therefore, to protect their potential as well as actual progeny, the retarded ought to be sterilized without their consent, since informed consent on their part is impossible. A second highly paternalistic argument for sterilization of retarded women in particular asserts that it is in their own best interest: menstrual periods and pregnancy represent unnecessary burdens on sexually active retarded women, and by sterilizing them, society frees them from these emotional and physical burdens.

A third, utilitarian theme that appears in some of the proposed legislation is directed toward women on public assistance. Welfare recipients unable to control their fertility represent, it is argued, a drain on taxpayers. Legislators in at least ten states have proposed coerced sterilization to relieve the government of what is perceived to be an unfair burden—namely, caring for children whose parents lack the responsibility or financial ability to raise them. Although none of the bills based on this argument have passed, persons on public assistance remain vulnerable. General public sentiment favors such measures, and because many of the targets of such legislation are members of minority groups, the situation is politically explosive.

There are allegations that welfare workers have threatened recipients with loss of benefits unless they agree to be sterilized. If the estimate of 200,000 federally funded sterilizations a year is accurate (Sewell, 1980), it would seem certain that many had been coerced in some manner. Reportedly, women have been sterilized without their knowledge while they were in the hospital for abortions or other surgeries. After passage of the 1970 Family Planning Act made sterilization available in federally funded clinics, reports of many such abuses surfaced. In response to the growing controversy, and in the absence of federal standards defining voluntary consent, the U.S. Department of Health, Education, and Welfare imposed in 1974 a moratorium on federal funding of sterilization of minors and persons considered mentally incompetent. A subsequent district court injunction permanently enjoined the government from sterilizing minors and incompetents.

The HEW Department also went a step further and imposed guidelines on the sterilization of all other public-assistance recipients. Individuals had to be informed of the nature, risks, and irreversible nature of sterilization. A waiting period of at least 72 hours was required between the written consent and the performance of the sterilization. Before consenting, the welfare recipient had to be informed that benefits could not be withdrawn for refusal to undergo the procedure. Furthermore, the sterilization required approval by a five-member review committee appointed by responsible authorities of the federally funded or sponsored program or project (e.g., Medicaid).

Despite these guidelines, Angela Davis (1981:220) argues that "the prevalence of sterilization abuse during the latter 1970s may be greater than ever before." The cutoff of federal funding of abortions and cutback of prenatal services for poor women are reinforcing traditional causes of abuse, she says: "There have been many more victims—women for whom sterilization has become the only alternative to abortions, which are currently beyond their reach. Sterilizations continue to be federally funded and free, to poor women, on demand" (1981:221). Sewell (1980:122) also emphasizes that sterilization abuse "impacts on minority and poor women," especially Hispanics, Blacks, and Native Americans, and contends attitudes of health providers reinforce the practice of discrimination by race and social class.

The availability of safe, effective, yet reversible sterilization techniques will arouse anew social pressures for nonconsensual sterilization. Since the procedure will no longer represent the permanent destruction of a person's reproductive capacity but, rather, a less intrusive and presumably temporary cessation of fertility, it will be less difficult to rationalize the forced sterilization of any human being, especially one for whom informed consent is not possible. From a purely technical standpoint, nonconsensual sterilization is more easily justified under such circumstances. However, the projected reversibility of sterilization also threatens to *increase* its use for eugenic or social control purposes by eliminating its most offensive aspect.

Opponents of compulsory sterilization have long emphasized the irreversible nature of sterilization in their arguments *(Skinner v. Oklahoma,* 1942). Will the new reversible techniques also reverse the trend toward more stringent restrictions? It may seem easier to justify a reversible procedure, but who would decide when to "pull the plug" on a sterilized retarded woman? Is there much likelihood that a technically reversible compulsory sterilization would ever actually be reversed, or is just the possibility of reversal sufficient ethical justification of the procedure? Should the government pay the costs of reversing sterilization if it paid for or ordered the original procedure?

Given the public's negative attitudes toward those on welfare, the increased emphasis on the population problem, the scarcity of public funds for welfare programs, and the continuing concern for the competency of parents, the availability of reversible sterilization may well spark renewal of the widespread use of incentives (or coercion) to encourage (or force) sterilization of the poor, retarded, and those otherwise deemed unfit to raise children.

Instead of abating as innovations in reversible procedures are perfected, the public controversy surrounding sterilization will almost certainly intensify. Reversible sterilization is a prime example of a technology that offers considerable benefits but also complicates an already complex set of policy issues. It also demonstrates the delicate interrelationship between social trends and technological advances, as change in either realm produces pressures for change in the other.

Finally, the sterilization debate illustrates the difficulties in making meaningful social policy in response to the rapidly changing technical and social context of human reproduction. Such devices as removable silicone plugs promise to revise the traditional conception of sterilization as irreversible, but they will not resolve the difficult policy dilemmas inherent in nonconsensual sterilization. These developments in sterilization technology are bound to alter the context within which such policy is established—but in what way?

Summary

The technologies of human genetics and reproduction raise critical policy dilemmas that increasingly require public attention. On the one hand, these innovations promise to alleviate the individual and social costs of genetic disease and give us more control over the destiny of future generations. They allow us to alter the givens concerning what it means to be a human being. On the other hand, widespread use of these technologies expands considerably our ability to label and categorize individuals according to precise genetic factors—thus effectively minimizing the human aspects of humanhood. The capacity to predetermine the sex of progeny, to select the frozen embryo that best meets one's expectations for a child, and to use DNA probes to identify persons with undesirable characteristics can easily dehumanize us even while giving the appearance of expanding individual choice. Clearly, these technologies dramatize the ethical dimensions of biomedical policy decisions.

Government will have to decide what role to play in setting liability, safety, and confidentiality standards for reproductive services. Should responsibility for monitoring and regulating these practices be delegated to the medical community, specialized professional associations, or individual hospitals and clinics, or should the state intervene to ensure certain minimal standards of safety, efficacy, and privacy? The debate over who regulates the burgeoning reproductive industry is bound to escalate. In many cases governmental forays into these innovations—whether by courts, legislatures, or other bodies—will only intensify the controversy over what should be done and by whom.

To date, government reaction to dilemmas of human reproduction has been piecemeal and often contradictory. Because of legislatures' inability and/or unwillingness take clear policy initiatives, reproductive policy is being made through common law. One of the fastest growing areas of tort law centers on procreation, and, although the courts may be handling responsibly the cases they receive, they cannot establish consistent policy in an area as complex as human reproduction. Only a fragmented, inconsistent policy framework exists at the state level. National regulatory guidelines of some form are needed to help shape responsibly the growing human-fertility intervention services now being undertaken in the United States.

3 Prenatal Intervention

The distinction between reproductive technologies and prenatal intervention is not a clear one because some techniques such as gene therapy overlap the two stages. The policy issues in each stage, however, are distinct enough to warrant this division. Prenatal issues involve a human embryo or fetus, which some members of society view as a human being. The developing fetus's complete dependency on the mother also leads to difficult dilemmas when fetal well-being conflicts with maternal choice. This chapter examines some of the most sensitive issues arising at the prenatal stage.

Prenatal Diagnosis

Prenatal diagnosis has become an important component of clinical prenatal care and is now a medical standard for women known to be at risk for abnormal offspring (Verp and Simpson, 1985). Of the 3.6 million infants delivered in the United States annually (Fuchs and Perreault, 1986:76), about 0.5 percent will suffer from a chromosomal abnormality, 1 percent will have a dominant or X-linked disease, 0.25 percent will have a recessive disease, and about 9 percent will have an irregularly inherited disorder (Scriver, 1985:96). Although many genetic diseases are very rare, collec-

tively they represent a significant cause of infant mortality. In addition, between 30 to 50 percent of hospitalized children have diseases of intrinsic
origin (that is, birth defects, or genetically-influenced diseases). "Moreover,
these patients have 'chronic' disease; their stay in the hospital is longer than
average, and readmissions are more frequent than for patients of other
types of disease" (Scriver, 1985:98).

Of the many prenatal diagnostic technologies currently used in the
United States, by far the most common technique for detection of genetic
disorders in utero is amniocentesis. In this procedure, usually administered
16 to 18 weeks after the beginning of the last menstrual period, a long, thin
needle attached to a syringe is inserted through the lower wall of the
woman's abdomen, and approximately 20 cubic centimeters (cc) of amniotic fluid surrounding the fetus is withdrawn. The fluid contains live body
cells shed by the fetus. These cells are placed in the proper laboratory
medium and cultured for approximately three weeks. Then type identification of the chromosomes (karyotyping) is conducted to identify any
abnormalities in the chromosomal complement, as well as the sex of the
fetus. If indicated, specific biochemical analysis can be performed to check
for up to 80 separate metabolic disorders and approximately 90 percent of
neural tube defects. If a fetus is prenatally diagnosed as having a severe
chromosomal or metabolic disorder, therapeutic abortion is offered. Initial concern over the potential medical risks of amniocentesis has largely
dissipated. In one analysis of over 3,000 consecutive amniocenteses, the
authors concluded that prenatal diagnosis is "safe, highly reliable, and extremely accurate" (Golbus, Loughman, Epstein, Halbasch, Stephens, and
Hall, 1979:157).

Amniocentesis is now regarded as accepted medical practice, and several
successful lawsuits against physicians who failed to advise amniocentesis
for patients over age 35 have accelerated its use. By 1980, approximately
40,000 women per year were undergoing amniocentesis. Moreover, an
article (Adams, Oakley, and Marks 1982:493) in the *Journal of the American
Medical Association* on maternal age and births in the 1980s indicated that
demand for amniocentesis will increase because of the trend toward high
maternal age in the population. Approximately 85 percent of amniocenteses are conducted for chromosomal evaluation, about three-fourths of
them for women over 35 years of age (Verp and Simpson, 1985:22).

The reason for the emphasis on amniocentesis for women over age 35 is that the frequency of chromosomal abnormalities—especially the most common one, Down's syndrome—increases dramatically with maternal age. Of women having live births in 1980, 29 percent of those aged 35 and older, compared to 4 percent of younger mothers, underwent amniocentesis (Fuchs and Perreault, 1986:77). Previous birth of a child afflicted with Down's syndrome or another chromosomal abnormality, parental chromosome abnormality, and severe parental anxiety are other common reasons for chromosomal evaluation. The remaining 15 percent of prenatal diagnoses are performed because (1) previous offspring or close relatives had neural tube defects; (2) there is a possibility of a sex-linked disorder; or (3) both parents are carriers of the gene for an inborn metabolic disorder such as Tay-Sachs disease.

Amniocentesis also can be used to detect Rh incompatibility between the fetus and the mother. Early diagnosis coupled with treatment using Rh immunoglobulin (protein-carrying antibodies) has successfully reduced the frequency of blood diseases caused by incompatible Rh-factor pregnancies. This is one of the few cases in which amniocentesis leads to treatment of a disorder. Along with its diagnostic applications, amniocentesis can be used in the third trimester to estimate fetal maturation and prevent premature delivery via cesarean section. It can help doctors select the optimal time for intervention by providing valuable information as to the relative risk of delayed or premature delivery of the infant.

Another technique, even more widely used than amniocentesis, that has become indispensable in prenatal diagnosis is ultrasound or "pulse-echo" sonography. This procedure directs high-frequency, nonionizing, nonelectromagnetic sound waves into the pregnant woman's abdomen to gain an echo-visual image of the fetus, uterus, placenta, and other inner structures. Noninvasive and painless, it reduces the need for x-ray scanning procedures. Studies to date have found no harmful long- or short-term hazards to the fetus from diagnostic sonography (Office of Medical Applications of Research, 1984). Besides its use in conjunction with amniocentesis to determine fetal position, fetal age, and amniotic fluid volume, ultrasound also enables observation of fetal development and movement, as well as detection of some musculo-skeletal malformations and major organ disorders (Warsof, Cooper, Little, and Campbell, 1986:33). More sophisticated devices can show images of fetal organs, such as the ventricles and intestines, and, in some cases, identify Down's syndrome fetuses

(Benacerraf, Gelman, and Frigoletto, 1987). Ultrasound use is also essential in conjunction with fetoscopy or placental aspiration (both described below) and in fetal surgery (Quinlan, Cruz, and Huddleston, 1986:558).

According to one report, "some authorities believe that all 'high-risk' pregnancies should have at least one sonogram" (Department of Health, Education, and Welfare, 1979:39). However, in 1984 a panel of medical and scientific experts, although recognizing the present value of ultrasound in obstetrics and identifying 27 clinical indications where it can be of benefit, advised that "data on clinical efficacy and safety do not allow a recommendation for routine screening at this time" (Office of Medical Applications of Research, 1984:672). They further cautioned that ultrasound examinations performed solely to satisfy the family's desire to know fetal sex, to view the fetus, or obtain a picture of it should be discouraged. Given ultrasound's broad medical applications, though, its use will continue to expand. It appears that its fullest development and applications are yet to be realized.

Potentially, a wide variety of hereditary disorders, including hemophilia, sickle-cell anemia, and possibly Duchenne muscular dystrophy, not approachable via amniotic samples, might be identifiable through fetoscopy (Perry, 1985). Fetoscopy is an application of fiber-optics technology that allows direct visualization of the fetus in utero. The fetoscope is inserted in an incision through the woman's abdomen, usually under the direction of ultrasound. Although the fetoscope can examine only a very small area of fetal surface at a time because of current limitations in instrumentation, it can be moved around in the uterus so as to examine the fetus section by section. Fetoscopy is also used to sample fetal blood under direct observation from a fetal vessel on the surface of the placenta. This is accomplished by placental aspiration, which entails inserting a small tube into the uterus and aspirating a minute quantity of blood for diagnostic testing. Fetoscopy also has direct therapeutic use in intrauterine blood transfusions of fetuses with hemolytic disease (i.e., breakdown of red blood cells) and offers considerable potential for introducing medicines, cell transplants, or genetic materials into fetal tissues in order to treat genetic diseases.

Despite substantial progress in fetoscopy and fetoscopic aspiration in the last decade, both are still considered experimental because of the hazards they pose for the fetus. Increased rates of premature birth and a miscarriage rate of between 3 and 5 percent accompany these procedures, and these risks must be reduced considerably before fetoscopy can become routine medical practice. Nevertheless, fetoscopy unquestionably marks only the beginning of attempts at in utero treatment of genetic disease and fetal surgery.

Approximately 6,000 infants are born each year in the United States with neural tube defects, the majority equally divided between anencephaly, in which much of the brain is absent and spina bifida (Main and Mennuti, 1986:1). Although there is a 2 to 3 percent risk of the defect recurring after one affected pregnancy, over 90 percent of neural tube defects occur without prior indication that prenatal testing is warranted (Macri and Weiss, 1982:633). In 1973, however, an association between elevated levels of maternal serum alpha-fetoprotein (AFP) and open neural tube defects was reported (Brock, Bolton, and Monaghan, 1973). Since then, research on screening has proliferated.

The level of AFP is determined from either amniotic fluid or maternal serum collected between the fourteenth and twentieth week of pregnancy. At present, these tests can diagnose approximately 90 percent of neural tube defects. Because dynamic changes in AFP levels occur normally during this period of gestation, however, more critical control data and more advanced techniques for quantification are required. Also, since there is some overlap in the distribution of AFP levels in amniotic fluid and maternal serum between pregnancies with neural tube defects and normal pregnancies, a false positive diagnosis occurs approximately once in every 10,000 cases.

Although measurement of AFP in amniotic fluid samples taken from women at known risk for fetal neural tube defects is now recommended, mass serum AFP screening from unselected pregnant women is still seen as premature. The Food and Drug Administration's approval, in 1983, of diagnostic kits to test for neural tube defects aroused concern from both consumer groups and scientists. Primary objections focused on the high rate of false positives, the crude nature of the test, and the possibility that women will abort fetuses solely on the basis of this preliminary screening device when the actual probability of having an affected child is very low. The American Medical Association's Council on Scientific Affairs (1982: 1478) emphasized the need for "intensive statewide pilot" projects to discover the appropriateness and efficacy of screening in the United States. In contrast, Main and Mennuti (1986:16) concluded that "voluntary maternal serum screening should be offered to the general obstetric population in the United States." Another observer (Simpson, 1986:202) cautions, however, that such screening must be coupled with ultrasound examination and is suitable only for certain parents. In any case, both maternal serum AFP screening and amniocentesis to identify neural tube defects will become more common in the near future.

The prenatal diagnostic techniques available to identify fetal defects continue to expand. In the past few years many of these, including amniocentesis and ultrasound, have become routine clinical procedures. Chorionic villi sampling (CVS), in which a biopsy is taken via laparoscope from the placenta, provides much of the same information as amniocentesis, but at about nine weeks of gestation thus enabling first-trimester diagnosis (Elias, Simpson, Martin, Sabbagha, Gerbie, and Keith, 1985). CVS currently elevates the risk of spontaneous abortion, but as this technique improves it undoubtedly will replace amniocentesis as the preferred approach to obtaining genetic material for prenatal testing.

In most instances, these technologies enhance a woman's reproductive freedom by providing information that helps her decide how to manage the pregnancy. However, as in the case of with reproductive technologies, any procedure that can be undergone voluntarily might also be coercively imposed. If prenatal diagnosis were to become legally mandated, through imposition of tort liability on those persons whose failure to use it resulted in harm to the fetus, then its very availability could limit the freedom of women who chose not to use it. What if a woman at high risk for a Down's syndrome infant refuses to undergo amniocentesis and then has a child with that chromosomal abnormality? Will she be judged liable for the wrongful life of the defective infant? Will her action be seen as irresponsible? What if she undergoes amniocentesis, finds out the fetus is affected, but refuses on religious grounds to abort the fetus?

The dilemma becomes more immediate, though perhaps clearer, if therapy is available in conjunction with the diagnosis, as in the case of Rh incompatibility. In *Grodin v. Grodin* (1980), a Michigan appeals court recognized a child's right to sue the mother for failure to obtain a pregnancy test. The logic of this ruling implies that a child would also have legal recourse against a mother who failed to monitor her pregnancy and thus was unaware of threats to the child's health during gestation. As Robertson

(1983a:448) points out, "the issue in such a case would be whether the mother's failure to seek a test was negligent in light of the risks that the test posed to her and the fetus and the probability that the test would uncover a correctable defect." Of course, prenatal diagnosis could be directly mandated by state statute with criminal sanctions for women who fail to comply. According to Robertson, state authorities could justify such a statute on public-health grounds. Despite constitutional questions of invasion of bodily integrity and privacy, Robertson feels such a statute could meet a "compelling state interest" standard.

Fetal Surgery

Until the early 1980s, the only options available upon prenatal diagnosis of a fetal disorder were to carry the defective fetus to term or abort it. The use of blood transfusions to treat Rh incompatibility, which have been performed successfully since the early 1960s, was nearly the only exception to this rule. Now, however, three basic approaches to treating the endangered fetus have emerged. The first entails administering medication or other substances (e.g., biotin, digitalis, cortisone, or related hormone drugs) indirectly to the fetus through the mother's bloodstream. Second, timely delivery can be induced so that the infant's problem can be treated immediately outside the womb. The third, and newest approach, is direct treatment of the fetus in the womb. In utero surgery has been made possible by new developments in ultrasound, amniocentesis, and fetoscopy and also by sophisticated surgical instrumentation designed specifically for such intricate procedures on fetuses. As a result, a series of breakthroughs has occurred, beginning in 1981 (Ruddick and Wilcox, 1982).

The first reported fetal surgery was performed in April 1981, on a 31-week-old fetus twin suffering from a severe urinary tract obstruction (Golbus et al., 1982). In a similar case that same year, surgeons operating under ultrasound treated a urinary tract obstruction in a 22-week-old fetus by draining with a needle an accumulation of fluid from a large cyst that threatened the fetus's life (Harrison, Golbus, and Filly, 1981). Also under ultrasound, doctors at several locales have implanted miniature shunting devices in the brains of fetuses diagnosed as having hydrocephalus, a dangerous buildup of fluid in the brain (Rosenfeld, 1982). These shunts drain the fluid from the upper ventricles of the brain into the amniotic sac.

In one case, surgeons also inserted a four-inch-long value-control shunt to permit continued drainage during the remaining three months of pregnancy. Other applications of fetal surgical methods have drained a collapsed lung which became filled with fluid and removed excess fluid from the chest and abdomen of another fetus.

Perhaps the most dramatic type of fetal surgery involved the surgical removal of a 21-week-old fetus from the womb. While surgery was performed on the fetus to correct a urinary tract obstruction which would have been fatal, the amniotic fluid was removed and kept warm. After surgical correction of the defect, the fluid and fetus were returned to the womb and it was sewn closed. The team of research surgeons, from the University of California at San Francisco, who attempted this surgery after years of research on animal fetuses, declared it successful, although this particular infant died of underdeveloped lungs following his birth three months after the in utero surgery (Harrison, Golbus, Filly, Callen, Katz, Delorimier, Rosen, and Jonsen, 1982).

Although puncturing the heart of a defective five-month-old fetus and letting it wither is hardly as impressive or appealing as the above cases, this procedure, performed on a twin fetus, did assure the survival of the remaining twin, which otherwise would have been aborted (Kerenyi and Chitkara, 1981). In this widely publicized case, amniocentesis revealed that one twin had Down's syndrome while the other was normal. The 40-year-old mother decided to abort them both rather than to carry the Down's syndrome fetus to term. Instead, the puncture procedure was performed under ultrasound in the twentieth week of pregnancy. The court acted as a guardian for the normal fetus and permitted the procedure. After a blood test confirmed that the affected fetus had been killed, the woman gave birth to a healthy infant four months later. In at least nine published cases selective feticide has been performed on twins as a result of prenatal diagnosis (Philip and Bang, 1985:175). According to these authors (p. 171), the frequency of genetic disorders in women with twin pregnancies who underwent amniocentesis varied from 1 to 2 percent in seven studies. Thus, this procedure probably will become more common in the future despite the furor it has raised.

Notwithstanding these successes, it must be stressed that all in utero surgeries remain high-risk procedures, used only on fetuses in danger of dying before or soon after birth without the surgery. Also, development of effective treatment for many fetal disorders in the foreseeable future is still improbable. Furthermore, the threat of precipitating premature delivery or spontaneous abortion remains a severe constraint on all but the most routine in utero interventions, despite great strides in preventing those dangers. Risk also confronts the mother any time fetal surgery is attempted. A further ethical dilemma of fetal surgery is that saving a fetus who otherwise would die may in fact cause a seriously disabled newborn to survive.

As Rosenfeld (1982:22) declares, when the applause over the successes in fetal surgery dies down, "one must quietly consider the consequences." As fetal surgery becomes more commonplace, which it is certain to do, and as it is performed earlier in gestation, the status of all fetuses as potential patients will further complicate the issue of fetal rights. Fletcher (1981:310) feels that "improvements in fetal therapy will establish a stronger ground to protect the affected fetus's right to life" and that this will collide with the established ground for a woman's right to choice concerning abortion. Ruddick and Wilcox (1982:11) agree that "fetal therapy, especially lifesaving surgery, would seem to make it easier to respect" the fetal claim to the right to life. Although Elias and Annas (1983:811) view forcible medical treatment as "brutish and horrible," they concede:

> When fetal surgery becomes accepted medical practice, and if the procedure can be done with minimal invasiveness and risk to the mother and significant benefit to the fetus, there is an argument to be made that the woman should not be permitted to reject it. Such rejection of therapy could be considered "fetal abuse" and, at a late stage in pregnancy, "child abuse," and an appropriate court order sought to force treatment.

The Policy Context of Fetal Surgery

"The concept that the fetus may be a patient, an individual whose maladies are a proper subject for medical treatment as well as scientific observation, is alarmingly modern" (Harrison, et al., 1982). As noted earlier, the unique feature of fetal surgery is that it requires violation of the mother's rights to personal autonomy if she does not consent. No new legal problems arise unless the mother refuses to consent—in which case the legal dilemma is agonizing, especially if she desires to carry the fetus to term. In our society, the status of patient usually carries with it the notion of autonomy. But in these cases, whose rights take precedence: those of the fetus, or those of the mother whose body must be invaded in order to facilitate the surgery?

John Fletcher (1981:772) contends that "it would be unwise now in fetal therapy to close the issue between fetal interests and parental interests in favor of the fetus. As long as the fetus is not separate from the mother, choices about treatment ought to be made only with her informed consent." Concerned about fetal surgery's risks to both fetus and mother, Fletcher argues that fetal therapy will present "intense moral problems," particularly in borderline cases where the treatment endangers the mother more than the fetus. He concludes (1981:773) that "the most difficult moral dilemma in medical ethics in the United States in the near future will be the influence of cost considerations on the quality of treatment in borderline cases." Despite the conflict between fetal and parental rights and the substantial costs involved, the preventive nature of some fetal surgeries might make them justifiable on cost/benefit grounds.

As we have noted, those borderline surgical interventions in utero might also save a fetus whose prospects for meaningful life are minimal or nonexistent. In such a case, could a tort claim for wrongful life be filed on the presumption that the fetus would have died without the lifesaving surgery but now was forced to live? Or, conversely, could a mother or physician who refused to perform such surgery be successfully held negligent under such tort action? Ruddick and Wilcox (1982), anticipating these types of problems, recommend the use of therapeutic contracts where the woman, not the fetus, is the principal party to the therapy.

The rapidly developing advances in a variety of in utero treatments, including fetal surgery, accentuate a subtle but real shift toward recognition of the fetus as an independent self. Technologies that depict the growing organism as human, amniocentesis labeling that entity as a "boy" or a "girl," and prospects of a wide variety of direct surgical interventions certainly give the developing fetus status as an individual of some importance. While the fetus still cannot be described as a fully autonomous person, it is being granted broader human characteristics that lead toward a redefinition of parental responsibility to the unborn patient.

Although case law is primitive in this area, some precedents exist in which the courts have ordered procedures over the mother's objections solely to provide proper medical care for her unborn child. In *Jefferson v. Griffin Spaulding County Hospital* (1981) the Supreme Court of Georgia reaffirmed the principle of viability established in *Roe v. Wade* by determining that a third-trimester fetus's legal right to the preservation of its life overrides the religious freedom of the mother. In this case, Mrs. Jefferson refused to have a cesarean section on religious grounds, despite the medical indications that without it the chances of survival would be less than 10 percent for the infant and 50 percent for the mother (Poe, 1981). The superior court found that, as a matter of fact, the child was viable and fully capable of sustaining life independent of the mother. For the court, there were two persons with separable lives. However, the court also ruled that the mother could not be forced to present herself to the hospital. On the following day, the Georgia Department of Human Resources petitioned the juvenile court for temporary custody of the unborn child, alleging that the child was being deprived of proper prenatal care, and sought a court order requiring the mother to submit to a cesarean section. The court found in favor of the department and gave it full authority to make all decisions concerning the child, including consent for the surgical procedure on the mother. The Supreme Court of Georgia denied a motion filed by the Jeffersons to stay the superior court's edict, declaring that the state is the ultimate guardian of society's basic values and that the life of the unborn child takes precedence over the mother's religious beliefs. Ironically, Mrs. Jefferson left the area and uneventfully delivered a healthy baby without surgical intervention despite the physicians' predictions.

The *Jefferson* ruling sets a key precedent in defining the unborn's legal right to equal protection under the law. When the mother's actions are judged detrimental to the health or life of the potential child, courts have shown little hesitancy to constrain her liberty. Although in *Jefferson* the court spoke in terms of a state interest, it actually weighed fetal against maternal rights, placing upon the mother an enforceable legal duty to safeguard the fetus's life at the expense of her own constitutional rights. The court relied on *Roe v. Wade* (1973) to establish a state interest in protecting a viable fetus. According to Finamore (1982:87), however, this formulation "significantly transcends" the boundaries of *Roe* by enabling the state to compel medical treatment to save the life of the fetus. "This result," writes Finamore, "imputes rights to the fetus which are enforceable against the mother. It also creates a corollary duty on the part of the mother to safeguard the life and health of the fetus." Mrs. Jefferson's case also raises a serious question as to the extent to which the courts should defer to medical judgment in compelling medical care, since the prognosis given to the courts proved to be wrong.

The *Jefferson* decision relied heavily on the Supreme Court's viability distinction in *Roe* and authorized surgery to protect a nearly born fetus. But in utero treatment is also enabling surgery for fetuses defined in *Roe* as not yet viable. On what basis might the courts order these procedures? As long as *Roe* stands, the woman could evade a court order by having a legal abortion. However, what if she decides to carry the fetus to term but refuses to consent to surgery deemed necessary to protect it?

In *Taft v. Taft* (1983), the court was faced with a similar dilemma, though it did not involve surgery on the fetus itself. The husband of a woman in the fourth month of pregnancy sought a court order granting him authority to force her to submit to a cerclage operation, which involves suturing so that the cervix will hold the pregnancy until later in gestation. Although the mother wanted to have the baby, she refused on religious grounds to consent even though a physician testified she would miscarry without the procedure. The trial court granted the husband authority to give consent for the operation, but this decision was reversed on appeal by the Massachusetts Supreme Judicial Court, which noted that "no case has been cited to us, nor have we found one, in which a court ordered a pregnant woman to submit to a surgical procedure in order to assist in carrying a child not then viable in term." The court, however, did not rule out the possibility that the state might possess a sufficiently compelling interest in an unborn's life to outweigh the mother's right to privacy. The court stated: "We do not decide whether, in some circumstances, there would be justification for ordering a wife to submit to medical treatment in order to assist in carrying a child to term. Perhaps the State's interest, in some circumstances, might be sufficiently compelling . . . to justify such a restriction on a person's constitutional right of privacy." (*Taft v. Taft*, 446 N.E. 2d at 397).

These decisions regarding coerced surgery to protect the fetus leave many questions unanswered. What standards of care will the courts use, and where will they draw the boundaries? Would the courts come to similar conclusions with a 20-, 24-, or 28-week-old fetus, if doctors considered it medically viable? If the court can order a woman to undergo a cesarean section, can it not also order her to allow corrective surgery on her unborn yet viable fetus of 24 weeks or more? As a report by the President's Commission for the Study of Ethical Problems in Medicine and Biomedical and Behavioral Research (1982:66) suggested, "Further developments in gene surgery or gene therapy may lead to further departures from the principle that a competent adult may always refuse medical procedures in non-emergency situations and from the assumption that parenting and reproduction are largely private and autonomous activities."

Clearly, cases in which the mother's rights and the fetus's medical needs conflict will offer vexing legal questions in the coming years. The basic issue here is whether the fetus should be considered a patient separate from its mother. Prior to recent developments in fetal surgery, the fetus generally was considered a distinct patient, and certain defects were treated with medicines administered to the mother or directly into the amniotic fluid, but these procedures, though requiring the mother's cooperation, were not as physically intrusive as surgery. The dilemma in fetal surgery is that treatment necessarily entails invading the physical integrity and privacy of the mother, who must consent to surgery on herself for the sake of her unborn child.

Although many obstetricians prefer to view the mother and fetus as a single biological entity sharing interests which are furthered by proper maternal care during pregnancy, advances in fetal care which clearly differentiate the fetus from its mother for treatment purposes may make this perception untenable (Lenow, 1983:2). According to Bolognese (1982:13), as it becomes the subject of new treatments in the burgeoning field of perinatology, the fetus will gain more advocates within the medical community. This potential conflict between obstetricians representing maternal interests and perinatologists representing fetal interests could paralyze judicial deference to the medical profession's determination of viability.

Until recently, the courts were hesitant to recognize causes of action for prenatal injury because of the difficulty of demonstrating proximate cause and determining reasonable standards of care. Advances in medical technology and in knowledge of fetal development, however, are rapidly altering this situation. The availability of prenatal diagnostic techniques amniocentesis, ultrasound, and fetoscopy, along with advances in genetic screening and collaborative conception techniques, places increased pressures on parents to use these technologies. The most intrusive of these developments, fetal surgery, potentially pits the fetus's right to be born with a sound mind and body against the mother's right to autonomy. In addition to increasing recognition of the fetus as a person, these advances in medical science make prenatal injury cases similar to more conventional malpractice or injury claims.

The Fetal Environment: *Rights and Responsibilities*

The rapid expansion of knowledge regarding the environment of the fetus has been accompanied by a growing concern for providing the fetus as safe as possible a sanctuary in the womb. This emphasis, in turn, has led to new consideration of the mother's obligation to provide such an environment for the fetus. The concept dates back at least as far as Aristotle, who in his *Politics* (7, xvi, 14) exhorted pregnant mother to "pay attention to their bodies . . . take regular exercise, and follow a nourishing diet." But now significant scientific evidence is suggesting that particular behavior of the mother during pregnancy might endanger the life or health of the fetus. As King (1980:81) notes, this "increasing awareness that a mother's activities during pregnancy may affect the health of the offspring creates pressing policy issues that raise possible conflicts among fetuses, mothers and researchers."

To what extent should society actively ensure a proper environment for the fetus? Aristotle proposed strict state control over breeding and the conditions of pregnancy to back up his concern for the new generation of citizens. In contrast, respecting the traditional emphasis on parental privacy in reproductive matters, the U.S. legislatures and courts have generally avoided this dilemma to date by refusing to intervene. *Roe* offered no guidance whatsoever for resolving cases where a mother's treatment of her own body might cause harm to the unborn child. However, at least one woman has been indicted for child abuse for giving birth to a child addicted to heroin (*In re Baby X,* 1977). More such rulings are expected as the ability to identify causes of fetal environmental damage increases.

Associations between a large number of maternal behavioral patterns and deleterious effects on the fetus have been found. It appears that the most critical period of development occurs between the third and twelfth weeks of human gestation (Nishimura and Tanimura, 1976). However, each organ has its own critical period, and for some, such as the brain where cell proliferation does not cease until at least six to eight months after birth, sensitivity to environmental teratogenic (i.e., defect-causing) agents extends throughout the pregnancy. Although the exposure to potential teratogens later in gestation might not result in gross organ system abnormalities, it might still be associated with other serious dysfunctions.

Moreover, research on teratogens indicates a likelihood that most fetal defects are caused by the combined effects of a number of more subtle teratogens acting in consort rather than a "single-hit massive teratogenic action." Melnick (1980:453) goes on to say that a "simple one-to-one correspondence does not exist for birth defects." The problem is vastly more complex and the solution depends on unraveling the unique contribution of each of a multitude of intimately related factors.

Despite the complex nature of the fetal environment and the variation of effects any single stimulus might have on a specific fetus, the evidence demonstrates that maternal behavioral patterns and health status can impair fetal development in many ways and cause irreparable harm in some cases. Although the data are not always conclusive, it appears clear that maternal smoking, drinking, eating, and general lifestyle can and do affect the fetus. More specific knowledge of the effects of certain behaviors will increase the emphasis on the mother's responsibility to assure the fetus as normal as possible an environment throughout the gestation period. Unlike most other prenatal disorders, many of these threats to the fetus and newborn are completely avoidable. Hanson (1980:221) for instance, exclaims that the fetal alcohol syndrome is a "national tragedy made particularly poignant" because it is so preventable.

When we ask what right a child has to a maximally safe fetal environment and as normal as possible a start in life, we again, face a potential conflict of rights between the developing fetus and the mother. It is certainly a tragedy that in a country as affluent as the United States children continue to be born with birth defects caused primarily by the mother's lack of proper nutrition or her behavior during pregnancy. In a democratic society the primary responsibility remains the woman's. She alone has the direct link to the fetus and she alone makes the ultimate decision as to whether or not to smoke, use alcohol or other drugs, and maintain proper nutrition, and so forth. However, these problems also suggest a broad social responsibility to remove women from socioeconomic circumstances that endanger the fetus. Prenatal nutrition programs, health care, and education on these matters are matters of both private and public health.

The Fetus and Workplace Hazards

One of the most vivid and explosive policy issues surrounding the issue of fetal health concerns hazards in the workplace. Workplace hazards pose in another form the conflict between the mother's right to control her life and the fetus's need for as risk-free an environment as possible. Should a fertile woman be allowed to work in an environment that might endanger the health of her offspring? If so, how much risk to the fetus is allowable? Furthermore, workplace hazards pit two social trends against each other. Society's strong interest in preventing fetal deformity demands some exclusion of pregnant women from dangerous work environments. But society has been seeking to remove barriers preventing women from choosing their own careers. When these two goals conflict, as they do here, the issue becomes a critical public one.

The problem of workplace hazards to the developing fetus came to public prominence with the publication of an HEW-sponsored report on occupational health problems of pregnant women (Hunt, 1975). This report acknowledged the growing scientific evidence that occupational exposure to some chemicals can affect a woman's capacity to bear normal children. In response, many American companies removed women of childbearing age from their jobs and refused to hire women with childbearing capacity. In his survey, Rawls (1980) found unanimous agreement, among representatives of every major chemical company, that no woman biologically capable of bearing children should be exposed to substances that pose a direct risk to the health and viability of the unborn child. The Equal Employment Opportunity Commission (1980) estimates that ultimately 20 million jobs nationwide could be involved. Bayer (1982:15) argues that any effort to extend exclusionary policies to areas in which females represent a major segment of the labor force, such as health care, would cause major social disruption and unjustifiable harm to women workers.

This issue of employment policies and pregnancy is becoming more important as women of childbearing age join the labor force, especially as they enter traditionally male-dominated occupations in heavy industry where there is a substantial probability of exposure to toxins. The size of the population potentially at special risk is enormous (Furnish, 1980:122). Of the 25 million women of childbearing age in 1975, approximately 68 percent were working. The Occupational Safety and Health Administration (OSHA) estimated that one million of these women were working in occupations involving the possibility of exposure to chemical substances which could cause birth defects or miscarriages. Moreover, over a million babies a year are born to women who work while they are pregnant. Although most of these women have healthy babies, the population at risk is large and continually expanding.

Spokespersons for the industries with exclusionary policies have attempted to justify their action as necessary to protect the health of the developing fetuses. They argue that the potential fetus has a right to protection from injuries that might result if the mother is exposed to workplace toxins. Employers are also protecting themselves, of course—from potential liability should a fetus be affected by the teratogen or toxin. As we learn more about teratogenic and mutagenic (mutation-producing) effects of agents that are toxic for the fetus but not necessarily for the mother, the threat of such large damage suits increases. Therefore, the companies do have a reasonable economic interest in protecting themselves from that eventuality.

A number of companies have established policies that exclude all fertile women—not just pregnant women—from positions where the workers are exposed to high levels of potential toxins. This action is reasonable from a fetal development perspective because the most severe effects of teratogens often occur in the first month of pregnancy, sometimes even before the woman knows she is pregnant. In another sense, though, this class action approach is an overkill, because many women of reproductive age do not plan to have any children or have already completed their families. This fact has led to an even more controversial proposal—to permit a woman to retain her high-risk job only if she agrees to be sterilized. Other women have been offered a lesser assignment outside the high-risk environment.

Not surprisingly, civil libertarians and feminists have attacked these exclusionary policies. Petchesky (1979) contends that the recent focus on fetal rights brings us back "to the Victorian notion that a woman's childbearing capacity . . . should determine where and whether she may work." Bayer (1982) supports stronger measures to lessen overall toxin levels in high-risk industries and guaranteed job security for women in such positions, despite the potential risk to their progeny. He also provides evidence that many of these industries have exaggerated the dangers of workplace hazards to fetuses in framing their exclusionary policies. Despite these objections by advocates of women's right to work, however, concern for fetal welfare is growing. Bayer's emphasis on making the workplace environment safe for all employees, thereby eliminating the need to discriminate by status or sex, has little chance of making significant headway in the near future, especially in industries, such as health care, where the hazards are largely unavoidable.

Although Howard (1981:836) rejects the "romantic paternalism" inherent in industries' attempts to protect women by excluding them from high-risk positions, she argues that these objections do not demonstrate satisfactorily that any employee has the right to assume the risk of fetal as well as personal injury:

> But when fetal health is implicated, sex-based discrimination may well be excusable. Given the social and economic costs of producing and caring for defective children and the substantial likelihood that the employment of workers in unhealthful environments will result in the birth of such children, it is justifiable to exclude some members of one sex from a very narrow class of industries in order to prevent this outcome—as long as the exclusion is in fact narrowly tailored, objectively applied, and based upon credible scientific evidence.

But what constitutes "credible scientific evidence" and "objectively applied" exclusion? And, most importantly, who decides: the woman, the employer, the government?

Unfortunately, it is extremely difficult to specify the extent to which environmental factors harm the fetus because, when two or more agents interact, their individual impact is very hard to isolate. Also, many of the conclusions are based on epidemiological studies, which give statistical but not causal evidence of correlations between maternal behaviors and fetal defects. Statistical data are amenable to varying interpretation depending on the perspective of the user, thereby resulting in conflicting conclusions. In spite of the difficulties of proof, however, a growing body of evidence has strengthened the hypothesis that toxic environmental factors cause fetal harm. According to Eula Bingham (1980:5),

> the more we learn about the effects of environmental toxic exposures on reproduction, the more we suspect that it is a substantial burden. The list of chemicals and other toxic substances such as radio frequency microwaves grows almost daily as our research efforts expand. NIOSH (the National Institute for Occupational Safety and Health) now lists 56 substances which are mutagenic in animal tests and 471 teratogens.

An increasing number of research studies have found ties between selected chemical and physical agents in the workplace and fetal injury or death (Valentine and Plough, 1982:147).

Although the precise manner in which many chemicals affect the fetus is still unknown, physical evidence of the devastating impact of a number of substances is accumulating. Toxic substances can harm the fetus either indirectly, by altering the parents' genetic material or reproductive system, or directly, by affecting the developing fetus in utero. Mutagenic agents alter the chromosomal structure of the parents' germ plasm, while teratogens can operate directly on the fetus to cause malformations. Furthermore, while long-term intergenerational effects are very difficult to ascertain, certain carcinogenic agents appear capable of acting on the cells of the fetus and eventually leading to cancer in their offspring.

In 1987 the National Institute for Occupational Safety and Health's Registry of Toxic Effects of Chemical Substances contained entries for over 79,000 chemicals. It cited data on the reproductive impact for over 15,000 of these chemicals, though the quality and accuracy of the citations were not evaluated. Of the 2,800 chemicals evaluated in animals for teratogenicity, 38 percent exhibited some teratogenic potential. To date approximately 40 agents are recognized as human teratogens (Larsen and Greendale, 1985). One agent with well-documented links to fetal damage is lead. The incidence of spontaneous abortions and stillbirths among female workers exposed to excessive lead levels is abnormally high, and the children of such workers are unusually susceptible to convulsions after birth. Maternal exposure to elevated environmental lead levels during pregnancy has been correlated with mental retardation and neurological disorders in the offspring (Rom, 1980). Mercury, too, is known to pass through the placental barrier and cause damage to the fetus's central nervous system, resulting in retardation, palsy, and seizures as well as heightened rates of stillbirths (Smith, 1977).

Many other substances widely used in industry are known or suspected to have adverse effects on the reproductive systems of exposed workers. Chromosomal damage has been reported in workers exposed to benzene, a solvent found in paint strippers, rubber cement, nylon, and detergents. Anesthetic gases produce miscarriages and birth defects in the progeny of both male and female operating-room and dental personnel (Cohen, 1980). Exposure to chlorinated hydrocarbons, used to manufacture dry-cleaning fluid and other general solvents and pesticides, can cause serious fetal damage (Howard, 1981). Exposure to vinyl chloride has been tied to severe impairment of the reproductive system, abnormal rates of miscarriage, and chromosomal damage to fetuses.

In addition to these substances, other agents have been linked to fetal harm. Ionizing radiation can cause substantial fetal damage, especially to women working in the health industry. Communicable infections crossing the placental barrier can cause spontaneous abortion, fetal infection, or fetal abnormalities, of which hepatitis is the most common. The incidence of neonatal (i.e., at or just after birth) hepatitis rises to nearly 77 percent when the mother becomes infected during the third trimester or shortly after delivery, while incidence is only 10 percent if the mother is infected in the first or second trimester. Also, infants in nurseries transmit rubella, a teratogenic virus, to nurses and attendants (Hunt, 1978:76).

Although nearly all agree that exposure of the pregnant woman to toxic agents is the most direct workplace threat to the developing fetus, there is growing evidence that fertile males also might contribute to fetal damage. This possibility is critical for public policy. Policies that discriminate against women of childbearing age might be justified under some circumstances if the prime or only source of harm for the fetus is through the mother. If, however, the effect of these agents on the male reproductive system also harms the fetus, then the current policy focus on workplace hazards to women is misplaced (Williams, 1981:704). To date, corporate policies have centered on the maternal contribution to fetal health and have failed to consider the male role, which is finally receiving attention in reproductive research.

According to the Council on Environmental Quality (1981:3), there is at best a limited scientific basis for treating men and women differently because of potential adverse effects on the fetus. More research on the potential contribution to fetal damage caused by male worker exposure to teratogens or mutagens is crucial for analysis of employer policy. Clearly, if a toxic substance can reach a fetus with equal frequency through its male or female parent, any policy that excludes only women from working with that substance discriminates unjustly. Although attention, especially concerning teratogenic agents, is bound to focus primarily on women, the issue of workplace hazards demands much more research on males as well as females.

Government Action on Workplace Hazards

In October 1978 Congress passed the Pregnancy Discrimination Act, which included the Pregnancy Amendment to Title VII of the Civil Rights Act. This amendment left no doubt of Congress's intent to include discrimination on the basis of pregnancy as a clear case of sex discrimination. The Act stated that "women affected by pregnancy, childbirth, or related medical conditions shall be treated the same for all employment-related purposes . . . as other persons not so affected." According to Furnish (1980:65), this amendment ensured a clash between the law and two distinct interest groups: employers intent on excluding pregnant women from particular jobs, and pregnant employees who wished to be excused from particular jobs temporarily. Mattson (1981:33) criticizes the act for disregarding "the potential for harm to the unborn in certain working environments." The Pregnancy Discrimination Act extended the scope of Title VII to the whole range of matters concerning the childbearing process, but it gave virtually no consideration to the issue of fetal vulnerability to workplace hazards.

In *Wright v. Olin* (1982), the Fourth Circuit Court became the first appellate court since this 1978 amendment to hear a Title VII sex discrimination suit grounded on the pregnancy-based distinction. The court clearly made an effort to reconcile Title VII and fetal vulnerability to workplace hazards. It attempted to answer the question: under what circumstances and on what basis can employment practices avowedly designed to protect unborn fetuses from workplace dangers be justified despite their "disproportionate adverse impact upon women's employment opportunities"? In this case, the plaintiffs brought a class-action suit charging that certain practices and policies of the employer violated Title VII. Prominent among these alleged violations was the defendant's "female employment and fetal vulnerability program" that excluded women from some jobs and restricted access to others solely on grounds of pregnancy or fertility.

The trial court concluded that the program did not violate Title VII. Reversing the district court's decision, the circuit court conceded that the fact situation before them did not "fit with absolute precision" into any of the developed theories of Title VII claims and defenses. While the court agreed that the plaintiffs had established a prima facie case of Title VII violation which could be rebutted only by a business-necessity defense, it rejected the argument that all classifications based on pregnancy constitute disparate treatment for women. The court held that an employer may impose otherwise impermissible restrictions on employment opportunities for women if the restrictions are reasonably necessary to protect the health of female employees' unborn children from workplace hazards. However, the circuit court ruled, in sending the claim back to the district court, that if the Olin Corporation wished to assert the business-necessity defense in a manner consistent with the circuit court's guidelines, it would have to prove that protecting fetuses from exposure to toxic substances requires restrictions on female, but not male, employees. As we have seen, based on current scientific knowledge, that is not an easy task.

According to Ashford and Caldart (1983:562), industrial control of reproductive hazards can come about in two principal ways: industry will change either on its own, in response to economic constraints, or in compliance with government regulation. They note that "Reproductive hazards potentially can be regulated by a variety of federal agencies. The most likely sources of regulation are the EPA (Environmental Protection Agency) under TSCA (Toxic Substances Control Act) and the air, water, and pesticide acts; the Food and Drug Administration under the Food, Drug, and Cosmetic Act; the Consumer Products Safety Commission under the Consumer Products Safety Act; and OSHA under the OSH Act." Although Furnish (1980) doubts that regulation by either these agencies or the Equal Employment Opportunity Commission will resolve the dilemma posed by Title VII and fetal vulnerability to toxic work environments, the present regulatory confusion does demonstrate the difficulty of reconciling interests through political mechanisms.

In 1980, OSHA concluded that exclusionary policies, such as those imposed against pregnant women, undermine the principle that the workplace should be a safe environment for all persons. Instead of discriminating against women of childbearing age or coercing them into ending their fertility, OSHA declared, industries should set exposure standards that take such vulnerability into account. In other words, OSHA argued that high-risk industries should not be able to reduce their liability for damage awards by excluding classes of workers. Moreover, no worker should be forced to sacrifice her reproductive rights in order to hold her job.

Earlier, OSHA had become embroiled in the case involving the American Cyanamid's exclusionary policy, under which five women were sterilized at the company's Willow Island, West Virginia plant in order to keep their jobs. In April 1981, after considerable administrative litigation, the Occupational Safety and Health Review Commission dismissed OSHA's citation against American Cyanamid's fetus-protection policy. The majority decision declared that the choice of sterilization is not the product of corporate policy but rather "grows out of economic and social factors which operate primarily outside the workplace" (Secretary of Labor v. American Cyanamid).

Late in the Carter administration, OSHA, the Equal Employment Opportunity Commission, and the Office of Federal Contract Compliance Programs prepared quidelines to regulate these corporate policies. These guidelines, which focused on the woman's right to control her reproductive capacity and employment, would have tolerated exclusionary policies for pregnant women only as a last resort. Also, such protective actions would be temporary, pending full examination of systematic research on workers' contributions to fetal harm. Due to opposition on both sides—from a broad variety of business groups concerned with governmental intrusion and from feminist and trade-union groups that argued that the guidelines were not strong enough—the proposed regulations were politically vulnerable. The Reagan administration's decision to withdraw the proposed guidelines was no surprise (Bayer, 1982:18).

The ongoing controversy over protection of the fetus from workplace hazards vividly illustrates the conflict between women's rights to employment and reproductive autonomy and concerns for the rights of those yet unborn. Does the state have such an overriding interest in protecting future generations as to permit employers to exclude females of reproductive age from a workplace environment if there is sufficient medical evidence of possible fetal harm? If so, what constitutes "sufficient" medical evidence? Conversely, do civil rights laws protect women from such exclusionary practices? Who ought to bear the burden of protecting potential children from workplace toxins: all potential mothers (by losing their jobs), or industry (by either reducing toxins to levels safe for the unborn or assuming liability for children born with problems caused by workplace teratogens)?

Some balance must be struck between these competing claims. Although Valentine and Plough (1982:154) are correct in their conclusion that present scientific uncertainty about reproductive hazards casts doubt on the wisdom of strong regulation at present, women should be assisted in protecting their unborn children while not having to sacrifice their jobs. Women should be entitled to assurances of job security, seniority, and wages during pregnancy, along with temporary transfers to lower-risk positions. The present "either-or" mentality, in which many women are forced to choose between children and career, must be overcome.

Embryo and Fetal Research

Another policy area of growing importance, pitting the opportunity for valuable research against strong moral objections toward such research, centers on experimentation using human embryos and fetuses. Controversy focuses, not only on the ethical appropriateness of this research, but also on how much of society's resources should be used to experiment on subjects which cannot consent. Although human fetal research has always elicited controversy, most of the recent attention has centered on the use of spare embryos from in vitro fertilization or human embryos created specifically for research purposes.

Fetal Research

Fetal research has been praised as a "source of considerable medical progress" (Maynard-Moody, 1979:197). It has helped to clarify our understanding of human fetal development and of developmental disorders. Fetal research has also led to many innovations in diagnosis and monitoring of the fetus in utero, thus saving the lives of high-risk fetuses. It has provided improved life-support techniques for premature babies. Finally, it has resulted in broadened knowledge of the relative risk of drugs and vaccines on the fetus at various stages of development.

Despite these valuable contributions to biomedicine, however, human fetal research remains intensely controversial. At least 15 states have laws prohibiting or regulating fetal research, and a moratorium on federal funding of live fetal research existed during much of the 1970s. Upon coming to power in 1980, the Reagan administration moved slowly in appointing members to the National Ethics Advisory Board, which must approve any federal funding of fetal research. Moreover, federal regulations have discouraged most forms of fetal research over the last decade. For instance, research on a fetus scheduled for abortion is permitted only if it does not change the date or method of abortion and could still be performed safely even if the mother changed her mind and carried the fetus to term. Women may not be offered financial inducements to have an abortion for research purposes, and it is questionable whether researchers can even provide a free abortion in exchange for a woman's consent to allow experiments on the fetus she is aborting. In short, the legal atmosphere of fetal research is inhibiting, if not hostile.

One problem in analyzing fetal research is that it encompasses an incredible variety of types. To provide some orderliness, the National Commission for the Protection of Human Subjects of Biomedical and Behavioral Research (1975:7–15) sponsored an extensive review of the scientific literature. The Commission arrived at four broad categories of fetal research. Although new directions of research have emerged since that report was drafted, the categories remain meaningful. They separate fetal research into experiments involving dead fetuses, nonviable live fetuses in utero, viable live fetuses in utero, and fetuses ex utero.

According to Walters (1975:8–7), there are four major positions regarding the ethics of research on live nonviable fetuses before, during, or after induced abortion:

1. Nontherapeutic fetal research should not be done under any circumstances.

2. Nontherapeutic fetal research should be done only to the extent that such research is permitted on children or on fetuses which will be carried to term.

3. Greater latitude should be allowed for nontherapeutic fetal research than for research on children or on fetuses which will be carried to term. However, certain types of experimental procedures should not be performed.

4. Any type of nontherapeutic fetal research may be legitimately performed.

Resolution of this heated debate will require considerable specification the of the conditions under which proper research might be undertaken. Given the intensity of opinions on either side of the issue, moderating positions 2 and 3 seem most likely to gain general acceptance.

Despite disagreement over the need for human fetal research and a lack of consensus as to who benefits from the research, the fundamental question is whether a fetus at a particular stage is a person or not. Ramsey (1975), a proponent of position 1, declares that all research on live fetuses should be prohibited out of reverence for human life. He asks who can give appropriate consent to nontherapeutic fetal research and rejects the argument that a mother who is aborting a fetus can legitimately do so. For Ramsey (1975:89) the mother voluntarily waives any claim she had over the fetus once she has decided on an abortion. Hellegers (see Fletcher 1979:96) adds that "no one can give consent to an experiment on [a live] aborted fetus. . . . It would be like asking consent from a parent who had abandoned or battered a child."

For Joseph Fletcher (1979), on the other hand, live fetal research is morally justified if the benefits outweigh the costs. He opts for quality of life over quantity and contends that the elimination of fetal research would "paralyze our standards of reproductive medicine." To Fletcher (1979:96) the nonviable fetus is not a patient because it is not a person, and the only human subject to be protected in clinical experimentation and research is the pregnant woman. The fetus for Fletcher is an object of research not a subject; it is a non-personal organism that has value only when the mother desires that it be born. Therefore, no research on any not-yet-viable fetus, either in utero or ex utero should be regulated. Fletcher is critical of the federal government's temporary policy, in the 1970s, of banning ex utero experimentation on live fetuses as well as some provisions of the 1972 Peel report in Britain, which described fetuses as a new class of human subjects in need of protection through restrictions on acceptable research. As a result of his views concerning the status of the fetus and his situation-ethics moral persuasion, Fletcher views any type of fetal research as justifiable, depending on the "clinical situation and the design." He approves (1979: 104) of any use of "abortuses or dead fetuses—whole, tissues, or uterine materials—whether from voluntary or therapeutic abortions, with or without maternal consent."

Although Fletcher and Ramsey have eloquently articulated the extreme moral positions, most of the policy debate over fetal research has centered on refinements of more moderate stances. While the considerable benefits derived attract support for the research, a consensus on the need to keep it within narrowly defined boundaries also appears to be evolving. Policy issues now focus on what the boundaries will be—what constraints ought to be placed on fetal experimentation and who has appropriate decision-making authority.

Walters (1975:10) notes that public policy in a pluralistic society requires accommodation of a variety of belief systems and interests rather than the elevation of any single group's views to the status of national policy. Therefore, he recommends a moderate policy that allows nontherapeutic fetal research only to the extent that such research is permitted on children or fetuses that will be carried to term. He offers three parallel propositions (1975:11):

1. Nontherapeutic research on children should be permitted, if such research involves no risk or only minimal risk to the subjects.

2. Nontherapeutic research on fetuses which will be carried to term should be permitted, if such research involves no risk or only minimal risk to the subjects.

3. Nontherapeutic research procedures which are permitted in the case of fetuses which will be carried to term should also be permitted in case of (a) live fetuses which will be aborted and (b) live fetuses which have been aborted.

As noted earlier, both the Peel Report in Britain and the National Commission for the Protection of Human Subjects in the United States took a moderate approach in framing their policy recommendations. The U.S. Commission declared (1975:63) that its duty was to "specify the boundaries that respect for the fetus must impose upon the freedom of scientific inquiry." It judged the general principles for research on human subjects to be valid and binding for live-fetus research. These principles are: (1) to avoid or at least minimize harm whenever possible; (2) to provide for fair treatment by avoiding discrimination between classes or among members of the same class; and (3) to respect the integrity of human subjects by requiring informed consent. With regard to fetal research in particular, the Commission includes an additional principle: to "respect the human character of the fetus." Before a fetus is used for research, (1) prior investigations using animal models and nonpregnant humans must have been completed; (2) the knowledge to be gained must be important and unobtainable by reasonable alternative means; (3) the risks and benefits to both the fetus and the mother must be detailed; (4) informed consent must be sought and granted under "proper conditions"; and (5) subjects must be selected so that the risks and benefits are not biased along racial, ethnic, or economic lines.

According to the Commission (1975:74), nontherapeutic research on the fetus during an abortion procedure and nontherapeutic research on a nonviable fetus ex utero present special problems because they extend the life of a dying subject. These types of research are permitted only if (1) the fetus is less than 20 weeks old, (2) no significant procedural changes are introduced into the abortion procedure in the interest of research alone, and (3) no intrusion into the fetus is made which alters the duration of life. They must also meet the criteria for other categories of fetal research.

Court Reaction to Fetal Research

At least three federal courts have examined statutory provisions regulating research on live-born fetuses and have concluded that such laws do not violate any constitutional right. In *Wynn v. Scott* (1978), the appeals court reviewed an Illinois statute stating that "no person shall use any fetus or premature infant aborted alive for any type of . . . experimentation either prior to or subsequent to any abortion procedure except as necessary to protect or preserve the health and life of any such premature infant aborted alive." The court concluded that these provisions did not impose any burden on the woman contemplating abortion, nor did they pose any obstacle to the attending physician. Also, since the provisions do not infringe on a fundamental right, they are "subject to a less demanding test of rationality." Similarly, *Charles v. Carey* (1979) largely sustained Illinois's prohibition of fetal experimentation. The court did, however, invalidate a sentence in the statute that prohibited testing, for the purpose of confirming the physician's in utero diagnosis of genetic complications, of a fetus whose death resulted from induced abortion. According to the court, that one provision interfered with the "privacy right in procreation," which includes family planning.

A similar decision was handed down several years earlier in *Planned Parenthood Association v. Fitzpatrick* (1975). In this case, the court conceded that the authority to make regulations concerning the disposition of live fetal tissue was within the ordinary "general powers of the Department of Health, which are extremely broad" (Wardle, 1980:196).

Experimentation with Human Embryos

Although embryo experimentation has not yet raised a response like that to live fetal research, debate will intensify as intervention at the earliest stages of human development accelerates. The morality of experimentation on embryos remained an academic question when none were available. However, the successes of in vitro fertilization, especially in conjunction with superovulation techniques (which produce an exceptional number of eggs at one time), have resulted in the capability to fertilize large numbers of eggs, not only for transfer to the uterus but also for laboratory research. In addition, techniques designed to flush early embryos from the reproductive tracts of consenting women will assure an adequate number of laboratory specimens for any permissible research endeavors.

The goals of embryo research are broad in scope and the project gains in knowledge concerning infertility, contraception, malignant tumors, teratogens, chromosomal abnormalities, abnormal cell growth, and cell differentiation are impressive. Short (1978) suggests that embryo researchers should also assess in vitro fertilization itself to determine whether that process produces a higher incidence of embryonic abnormalities than the conventional method of reproduction. Short (1978:8–10) contends that if in vitro fertilization does in fact lead to an excess of abnormalities, it would be preferable to discover that excess in the laboratory rather than at the time of amniocentesis or birth. Conversely, Biggers (1978) argues that animal experimentalism is suitable for most questions concerning human reproduction and should be used where at all possible. Women, he says, should not be subjected to the risks of such research, and valuable human ova and embryos should not be used for laboratory research unless there is no reasonable alternative.

In February 1982, Steptoe and Edwards, who four years earlier had reported the first live birth through in vitro fertilization, created another worldwide tumult by referring to plans to freeze spare human eggs or embryos for future clinical or laboratory use. These materials were the result of superovulation. After selection of the most normal looking eggs for in vitro fertilization and embryo transfer, the extra eggs could either be retained for a later try at pregnancy or destroyed. Edwards has asserted

(Williams and Stevens, 1982:314) that these spare embryos "can be very useful. They can teach us things about early human life which will help that patient and other patients." In other words, in addition to possible future use for the couple or for another woman who cannot produce fertilizable eggs, these materials have value for laboratory research.

Just as in the case of fetal research, the acceptability of embryo research rests on the status accorded the early human embryo (see Isaaks and Holt, 1987:19-23). Is such research compatible with the respect due the embryo, and, if so, do the potential benefits of such research outweigh the potential adverse consequences? If both these questions are answered affirmatively, then attention shifts to proper standards that should be instituted to (1) secure prior consent of the ovum donors, (2) set criteria for establishing the need for human research, and (3) develop methods of weighing risks against benefits in specific research proposals.

Kass (1978) also notes that one must distinguish between embryos deliberately created for research purposes and untransferred embryos remaining after multiple ova are fertilized and one is chosen for insertion into the uterus. He concludes that embryos should not be created solely for laboratory research purposes, nor should invasive or manipulative research be performed on already existing human embryos. Citing the continuity between embryonic and fetal development and the potential viability of the early human embryo if it is transferred at the proper time, Kass (1978: 11) contends that any other policy would symbolize the belief that early human embryos are nothing but "things or mere stuff." Kass clearly is advocating the proscription of all human-embryo research. Kass expresses a definite preference for allowing untransferred embryos to die instead of transferring spare embryos to women other than the donor or using them for laboratory research.

Grobstein has taken a more moderate position, claiming that "human cells, tissues, and organs that have no reasonable prospect of possessing or developing sentient awareness" are "human materials rather than human beings or persons" (1978:229). Scientific evidence suggests, he says (1982:6), that at least until the eight-cell stage a multicellular individual is not present. The cells continue to act as individual cells rather than cell-parts of a multicellular individual. Since individuals are usually defined as multicellular, it is "difficult to maintain scientifically that a person has come into existence prior to the eight-cell stage." Grobstein, therefore, concludes that the entire preimplantation period is a developmentally preindividual stage and that, up to that point, safety of the procedure ought to be the prime concern. Errors with human materials, he concedes, must not be tolerated.

Although discussion of embryo research has focused primarily on its moral aspects, the legal status of the preimplanted embryo also has been raised. In *Del Zio v. Presbyterian Hospital* (1978), a jury awarded $50,000 for emotional distress following the intentional destruction of a culture containing gametes from the plaintiffs. This ruling suggests that although the early embryo is not a legal person (*Roe v. Wade,* 1973), the donors' special interest in the embryo gives it a legal value if not a legal status of some sort. Despite this single decision, Katz (1978:21-25) says it is unlikely that the destruction of preimplantation embryos will fall within homicide or anti-abortion statutes. However, Reilly (1977:214) warns that the embryo's legal status must be defined so that laboratory technicians and clinicians will know their legal responsibilities regarding the materials and products they handle.

4

Biomedical Issues within the Life Cycle

Although biomedical advances in human reproduction and the prenatal stage reflect the most revolutionary level of possibilities, interventions within the life cycle directly touch the lives of many more people and are thus of greater concern to most policy makers. Also, because many technological applications during the life cycle become, in effect, life-and-death decisions, often at great expense, they raise severe ethical and policy problems of their own.

This chapter focuses on several of the most dramatic applications of biomedicine within the life cycle. Neonatal intensive care, often fraught with controversy, is a logical starting point for our analysis. Organ transplantation also crystalizes policy issues surrounding the allocation of medical resources because of its high concentration of resources (including money, blood, personnel, and time) on one individual and questions regarding the quality of life of survivors. Third, this chapter examines efforts to modify or control behavior through medical interventions, including drug therapy and psychosurgery. Finally, we discuss an issue that underlies all these intervention possibilities: the dilemma of human experimentation.

Treatment of Seriously Ill Newborns

In a press conference held to announce guidelines for infant bioethics committees (IBCs), Robert J. Haggerty, vice president of the American Academy of Pediatrics, asserted that the question of who decides how to treat newborns with severe disabilities and how those decisions are made "has become the moral issue of our time" (American Academy of Pediatrics, 1984:1). Ironically, it is medicine's new found capacity to intervene and save severely disabled infants that has produced these controversial moral and public-policy dilemmas. Until very recently, nature decided which infants would survive and which would die. Today, however, increasingly sophisticated neonatal treatment has put nature on the defensive, successfully saving infants from a variety of physical conditions that in the near past would have certainly been fatal. In some cases, the patients go on to lead fulfilling lives. In many others, though, the surviving infant's quality of life is so low as to raise doubts about the use of the life-saving treatment. The result, according to the President's Commission for the Study of Ethical Problems in Medicine and Biomedical and Behavioral Research (1983:198), is that

> medicine's increased ability to forestall death in seriously ill newborns has magnified the already difficult task of physicians and parents who must attempt to assess which infants will benefit from various medical interventions and which will not. Not only does this test the limits of medical certainty in diagnosis and prognosis, it also raises profound ethical issues.

Moreover, these ethical issues soon become policy issues because, for reasons discussed below, (1) a large proportion are paid for by public funds and (2) neonatal care is extremely expensive in comparison to its frequently marginal long-term benefit.

The Technological Context: Neonatal Care

In the decade between 1970 and 1980, the death rate of neonates (newborns in the first 28 days of life) in the United States was cut almost in half, the greatest proportional decrease in any decade on record. A significant portion of this improvement occurred among the smallest of infants, those with birth weights below 1500 grams. Among infants weighing between 1000 and 1500 grams, the survival rate has increased from 50 percent in 1961 to over 80 percent now. Furthermore, over half of live-born infants weighing less than 1000 grams now survive, compared to less than 10 percent in 1961. This impressive increase in the survival rate, however, has been gained at great expense, both monetary and personal. These costs are carefully scrutinized for each of the two general categories of newborns in which decisions as to the use of life-sustaining treatment must be made: low-birth-weight infants and infants with congenital abnormalities.

Approximately 230,000 infants per year, or 7 percent of all live births in the United States, are classified as having low birth weight. Although infants under 1500 grams constitute less than 1 percent of all live births in the United States, they account for almost 25 percent of all admissions to Neonatal Intensive Care Units (NICU) and half of all infant deaths (Office of Technology Assessment, 1981:11). Most low-birth-weight babies are premature, although some are small despite a normal gestation period. Premature birth is caused by a variety of factors, including poor maternal nutrition and cigarette smoking as well as many other aspects of the fetal environment. Failure to thrive, or growth retardation of the fetus in the uterus, is found more often in births to women from the lower socioeconomic groupings, particularly young, single, non-white mothers who lack proper prenatal care (Eisner, 1979).

Birth weight is strongly associated with illness and mortality in the neonatal period. The lower the birth weight, the more severe the effects. According to Shapiro, McCormick, Starfield, Krisher, and Boss (1980: 363), low-birth-weight infants are forty times more likely to die in the neonatal period than infants of normal weight (over 2500 grams) and five times more likely to die between one month and one year of age. Despite the vast recent improvement in survival rates, a large proportion of infants born weighing less than 750 grams still die. One recent study showed survival rates of 45 percent for infants in the 700- to 800-gram range and 8 percent in the 500- to 600-gram range (Bowes and Simmons, 1980:1080). Moreover, many of the survivors have severe long-term health problems. In summarizing a series of studies, Strong (1983:16) found that the percentage of survivors of 500- to 1000-gram infants who have a major handicap (such as severe mental retardation, cerebral palsy, major seizure disorders, or blindness) ranges from 7 percent to 30.2 percent. An additional 21.9 percent to 55 percent have some lesser degree of handicap (such as learning disabilities, hyperactivity, verbal delay, or minor hearing loss). The percentage of infants with normal neurological outlook varies from 5.6 to 29.1. Many of these problems develop because the very low-birth-weight babies have been deprived of a critical maturation period in the womb. Although the major organ systems are in place by 20 weeks of gestation, they remain immature in development and function. When the fetus is separated from the functional environment of the uterus and its natural life-support system, only aggressive medical intervention can sustain life.

The most common complication of premature birth is hyaline membrane disease, a consequence of immature lung development. Machine-assisted ventilation by means of respirators is used to counteract the insufficient oxygen supply caused by this disease, but lung disease is still linked with 50 to 70 percent of deaths among premature infants. Low-birth-weight infants are also at high risk for birth asphyxia, which can cause permanent brain damage of varying degrees. Hypothermia, hypoglycemia, retarded bone growth due to calcium deficiency, and a susceptibility to infections due to an immature immune system are also common. Severe jaundice can result from an immature liver, and underdeveloped kidneys and gastrointestinal tracts make feeding difficult at best. NICU specialists face massive challenges as they strive to maintain the delicate balance essential to proper development of the low-birth-weight baby outside the womb.

The second category of seriously ill infants is those inflicted with congenital abnormalities requiring major medical attention if the infant is to live. About 4 percent of the infants born in the United States have one or more detectable congenital abnormalities. Although these situations account for only a small fraction of the neonatal intensive-care cases, they dominate the discussion in the media (remember Baby Doe and Baby Fae?) as well as the literature. The most common among these abnormalities are neural tube defects (NTDs), such as spina bifida and anencephaly, and Down's syndrome. Neural tube defects occur in approximately 2 of every 100 live births in the United States. The most prevalent NTD, spina bifida, causes physical and/or mental disabilities that vary widely in severity and may involve many organ systems. This wide variation in seriousness can make decisions as to whether or not aggressive surgical treatment is warranted—and, if so, what treatment is most appropriate—exceedingly difficult.

Similarly, although individuals born with Down's syndrome are mentally retarded, the degree of retardation varies widely and cannot be determined in early infancy, when the decision to treat or not treat the patient is crucial. Further fueling the debate over treatment of defective infants, a significant minority of Down's syndrome children are born with a gastrointestinal blockage, congenital heart defects, or both. Although surgical treatment in these cases often is routine, as opposed to severe spina bifida where the results of surgery are uncertain, many parents and physicians reject intervention efforts that preserve this type of life. Survey research data (*Gallup Report,* 1983) show that the public is evenly divided: 43 percent support allowing a severely deformed baby to die, while 40 percent approve medical intervention to save its life.

Neonatology

In 1975 the American Board of Pediatrics gave the first neonatology certification examinations. Since then over 1,000 neonatologists have been certified. Paralleling the growth of this medical subspecialty, high-technology neonatal intensive-care units have opened across the country. Over 600 hospitals now maintain NICUs. Some, such as Children's Hospital in Denver, which welcomes afflicted babies born within a 700-mile radius, have become regional centers specializing in highly aggressive treatment of newborns with low birth weight, congenital abnormalities, or other problems. High-risk fetuses are frequently being transported to these state-of-the-art hospitals, which have the latest in intensive maternal, fetal, and neonatal technologies and equipment. Upon birth, the baby is resuscitated if necessary and sped to a NICU. Fetal monitoring is often used to identify prenatally fetuses at risk; upon identification of such, the mother is transported to a hospital with a NICU for immediate treatment. NICUs almost always initiate aggressive treatment when necessary, because neonatologists are trained to use technologies to save lives. The Office of Technology Assessment (1981b:15) estimates that 6 percent of live-born infants are admitted to NICUs, usually staying for eight to eighteen days. The total cost for NICU care in 1978 was approximately $1.5 billion.

Issues in Treating Seriously Ill Infants

The dependence on highly sophisticated and expensive neonatal intensive care illustrates our society's tendency to stress curative medicine and ignore prevention. A large proportion of the low-weight pregnancies are precipitated by controllable environmental factors, yet "efforts to treat the problem have gained support far in excess of efforts to prevent it" (Miller, 1984:553). Instead of spending relatively small amounts of money to educate pregnant women and to provide adequate prenatal care and nutrition, we continue to emphasize after-the-fact treatments that exact a very high toll on society, especially on those individuals directly affected. This point is critical, because many of the neonatal survivors have life-long diseases or handicaps which require a long-term, exhausting commitment to these infants after they leave the hospital. This less dramatic but crucial follow-up care never seems to attract the support from the medical community and public officials that NICUs have received.

I agree with Mathieu (1984:610) that it is "short-sighted and potentially disastrous to mandate sophisticated and costly medical care for severely handicapped newborns" without addressing the hard allocative decisions of who cares and pays for these children if they survive. Many of them will require extensive medical care throughout their lives. Ironically, some of the problems, including blindness, damaged lungs, and mental retardation, result directly from the life-saving respirator itself, and the nearly pure oxygen it forces into the under-developed lungs of severely underweight newborns. Are the parents expected to bear full responsibility for this subsequent care? If so, they should have the final choice as to whether to initiate aggressive treatment at birth. What if the parents are not equipped to care for them? Until now, the record of state support has been lacking. As the number of severely ill infants we save increases, we must be willing to expend considerably greater resources to care for them throughout their lives. Responsibility does not end once they cease to be newborns; rather, once aggressive medical treatment ends, aggressive social care is essential. Pitifully, while encouraging aggressive medical intervention for neonatals, we have actually cut funding for social programs designed to cover later, "downstream" needs of the infants we save.

Opposition to aggressive medical intervention to save the lives of severely ill infants comes from several quarters and is based primarily on either quality-of-life or cost-effectiveness considerations. Sylvia Schechner (1980:142), a pediatrician, suggests that such efforts be withheld for infants below 750 grams, since so many who do survive have such poor quality of life. The infant should be kept comfortable but no life-prolonging steps should be taken. Young (1983:18) agrees in opposing aggressive therapy in these cases unless "strong, countervailing medical or social reasons" can be offered. Instead, he says, we must strive for a better balance between extraordinary neonatal treatment and allocation of resources for the long-term care of the disabled. To that end, he advocates setting limits on "technological expansionism" and channeling resources into before-the-fact prevention of conditions that we are currently "inclined to remedy, ex post facto, by highly aggressive technology." William Kirkley (1980:873) also raises the question of cost effectiveness, asking if public funds might not promote society's interests better if put to uses other than treatment of very low-birth-weight infants? This question is a matter of public concern in part because a significant portion of the overall cost of caring for these infants is covered by Medicaid (Strong, 1983:16). The imposing economic and emotional pressures on the family of a severely disabled child also militate in favor of withholding treatment for infants whose prognosis is poor.

However, not all are convinced by these arguments. Carson Strong (1983:19) rejects cost-effectiveness justifications of denying aggressive treatment to defective newborns: "Vigorous lifesaving medical care is required in the best interests of the patients. In clinical decision making this consideration outweighs the financial burden to society, which ought to continue paying for this kind of medical care, out of considerations of justice." Although Strong contends that the decision to initiate aggressive treatment at birth does not commit us to providing continuous intensive care, it is very difficult to withdraw treatment once begun. Paul Ramsey (1970) argues, further, that we have a duty to maintain neonatal life, despite any social costs, because the newborn possesses humanhood. Diamond (1977) agrees that even the deformed child has the right to live and that parents and physicians cannot decide to terminate that right, which takes precedence over all others.

The right to decide whether to use medical interventions to save the life of the defective newborn has resided generally with the parents, in consultation with their physician. In actuality, the decision frequently is made unilaterally by the attending physician in the delivery room, based upon his or her medical judgment as to the infant's quality-of-life potential. The President's Commission on biomedical ethics found that the prevailing opinion in the medical community continues to support leaving such decisions to parents because they are the ones who must bear the preponderant burdens of the decision: "physicians confirmed that decisions to forego therapy are a part of everyday life in the neonatal intensive care unit; with rare exceptions, these choices have been made by parents and physicians without review by courts or any other body" (President's Commission, 1983:207). The American Medical Association agrees that "the decision whether to exert maximal efforts to sustain life should be the choice of the parents" (Judicial Council of the American Medical Association, 1982:9).

Seldom is treatment continued over parental objections, but frequently the parents seem to be swept along by the inertia of the medical decision-making process, in effect deferring to specialists' judgment. In contrast, seldom if ever has parents' demand for continued treatment been dismissed. Some parents, however, feel they have been pressured to accept physicians' advice to discontinue treatment. One report (Crane, 1975:76) suggests that health-care providers sometimes manipulate the situation for their own benefit: "Consultation with the family is used in part as a method of ensuring that they will accept the decision and not take legal action against the physician later. It is not considered appropriate for the family to make the final decision."

Government Involvement In Treating Disabled Infants

Events of the last several years have brought a new player into these life-death decisions, beginning with the Reagan administration's "Baby Doe" regulations. These regulations were a reaction to the well-publicized case of a Down's Syndrome infant with an incomplete esophagus who was allowed to die with parental consent. Issued in 1983 by the Department of Health and Human Services (HHS) under a federal law banning discrimination against the disabled (Section 504 of the Rehabilitation Act of 1973), they ensured that treatment would not be deliberately withheld from handicapped infants. A "hot line" was set up on which hospital staff and others were urged to report potential violations. The courts, however, struck down the original regulations and a modified version in May, 1984.

In September 1984, after months of emotional hearings and difficult negotiation, Congress passed a child-abuse bill (HR 1904, PL 98-457) which included controversial Baby Doe provisions. The bill requires states, as a condition of receiving federal child-abuse aid, to have procedures for responding, through existing state child-protection agencies, to reports of medical neglect of handicapped infants in life-threatening situa-

tions. Hospitals are encouraged, though not required, to establish committees to review such cases. The bill also delineates special circumstances
within which withholding treatment does not constitute medical neglect.
Doctors do not have to take heroic measures when treatment is "virtually
futile" in saving the infant's life, when the infant is "irreversibly comatose," or when the treatment itself is "inhumane." Obviously, the wording of these exceptions and the bill's references to "reasonable medical
judgment" are ambiguous and open to a variety of interpretations (Rhoden and Arras, 1985).

The Baby Doe provisions were backed by a coalition of medical, handicapped, and right-to-life groups and had strong support from the Reagan
Administration. In contrast to the American Hospital Association (AHA)
and the American Academy of Pediatrics (AAP), the American Medical
Association did not support the infant-care provisions, because it felt they
left no room for consideration of the quality of life severely disabled infants would face if kept alive indefinitely. The AHA would have preferred
to see the federal government stay out of this area, but they accepted the
final, compromise version of the bill over previous ones.

May 1985 brought further "Baby Doe" regulations, in the form of the
HHS Department's final rule implementing the Child Abuse Amendments. The wording of the regulations showed clearly that the Reagan administration intended to interpret the provisions of the bill as narrowly as
the courts would allow. The HHS regulations rigidly interpreted the act's
"medical indications" policy, again rejecting any consideration of subjective quality-of-life judgments.

On June 9, 1986, the Supreme Court struck down the administration's
Baby Doe rules *(Bowen v. American Hospital Association)*. In a 5-to-3 vote,
the Court ruled that the federal law prohibiting discrimination against
handicapped individuals in activities receiving financial assistance does not
give the Secretary of Health and Human Services the right to intervene in
decisions regarding medical treatment of handicapped infants. Justice
Stevens, writing the plurality opinion (Justice Berger concurred with the
judgment but disagreed with the reasoning), stated: "Section 504 does not
authorize the secretary to give unsolicited advice either to parents, to hospitals, or to state officials who are faced with difficult treatment decisions
concerning handicapped children." Opponents of the Baby Doe rules
hailed the decision as a return of discretion to parents and physicians, while

proponents viewed it as undermining the newborn's right to be treated aggressively. But, especially since state laws regulating intervention in cases of medical neglect were not affected by the decision, the extent to which it will affect the treatment of handicapped newborns remains to be seen.

Human Organ Transplantation

One of the most dramatic areas of medical technologies, and the most expensive on a per-case basis, is the transplantation of major human organs, primarily heart, lungs, liver, and kidneys. Recent extension of human organ transplants into the realm of artificial organs and cross-species organ transplants has raised serious policy dilemmas that are bound to become more intense. Organ transplants also offer an opportunity to analyze the implications of public policy because government has been directly involved, through subsidies of kidney transplants.

This section examines the technological advances that define the medical boundaries of organ-transplant surgery. It also summarizes the current debate over developing a policy of organ transplantation and its implications for health care in the United States. Because heart and kidney transplantation have been dealt with extensively elsewhere, the focus here will be primarily on liver transplants, although comparative data on other procedures are included.

Medical Parameters of Organ Transplants

Advances in surgical procedure, organ preservation techniques, tissue matching, and drug treatment have combined to accelerate the use and magnitude of organ transplantation. As survival rates have continued to improve, the demand for transplant surgery has multiplied. Patients are now lining up for new livers, hearts, kidneys, pancreases, and heart-lung combinations as their original organs fail.

In November 1987, three-year-old Tabatha Foster received a new liver, pancreas, small intestine and parts of a stomach and colon at Children's Hospital in Pittsburgh after her system failed. Multiple transplants of this scope will increase as more transplant centers develop the capabilities. Although the number of transplant candidates remains small, the demand for transplant surgery is potentially unlimited in a population willing to go to great expense to prolong life. Transplant availability has already expanded rapidly to keep up with this demand. The number of medical centers doing liver transplants climbed from 3 to 36 in four years, and the number of heart-transplant centers multiplied from 5 in 1982 to 71 in 1987. More than 180 medical centers are now performing some type of transplant surgery.

Table 1 presents data on transplant procedures in the United States. By far the most common transplant is the kidney. Its moderately low cost, its reimbursement through Medicare, and the relative availability of donor organs ensures continued expansion of that program. Kidney transplants are clearly the most routine, although even here, up to 20 percent of the transplant patients die within one year and about 40 percent die within three years. The potential costs of heart and liver transplants far exceed

T A B L E 1

Organ transplantation in the United States

	Kidney	Pancreas	Liver	Heart	Heart/Lung
First Transplant	1954	—	1963	1967	1981
Number Performed/1985	7,695	87	602	719	37
Cost	$25,000 to $30,000	$35,000 to $60,000	$135,000 to $250,000	$60,000 to $110,000	$100,000 to $300,000
One year survival -rate/cyclosporine	80–95%	35–40%	60–70%	75–80%	
Approximate Number of Centers (1987)	120	21	36	71	9
Estimate Number who could benefit per year	7,000	5,000	10,000	50,000	—

Sources: American Council on Transplantation

those of the kidney program, primarily because of the large initial cost of these procedures. Also, survival rates remain lower for heart and especially liver transplants. Although liver-transplant survival rates undoubtedly will rise, this surgery will continue to be more problematic because of the nature of the organ and the difficulty of obtaining suitable donor organs. Since each person has only one liver and one heart, the use of living donors is not an option as it is with kidneys.

The Cyclosporine Controversy

The most recent development that has substantially improved the survival rate of transplant patients is the introduction of the drug cyclosporine. Cyclosporine is one of the most potent and specific immunosuppressants discovered so far. Approved by the Food and Drug Administration in 1983 for routine use, it suppresses the body's natural immunity system and keeps it from rejecting the transplanted organ, which is alien to the system. Cyclosporine is unique in that, while it suppresses production of the white blood cells responsible for organ rejection, it does not grossly interfere with the activation of those cells which destroy bacteria.

Not only has cyclosporine dramatically reduced the incidence of organ rejection, but it also slows the process of those rejections that still do occur. As a result, episodes of rejection are less dangerous and easier to treat. Both "survival and rehabilitation have improved markedly in cyclosporin-treated patients" (Austen and Cosimi, 1984:1437). Cyclosporine has roughly doubled the overall one-year survival rate for kidney (from 50 percent to about 85 percent) and liver (from 35 percent to 70 percent) recipients. The Stanford University trial of cyclosporine in heart-transplant patients has proven its superiority over conventional immunosuppression. Stanford now projects that 75 percent of recipients will survive for at least two years, up from 58 percent without the drug. Also, accelerated rehabilitation has cut the average hospital stay from 72 to 42 days and hospital costs from over $100,000 to $67,000 (Austen and Cosimi, 1984:1437).

Despite its effectiveness in suppressing the immune system and in markedly improving survival rates, cyclosporine, like all medical innovations, has its disadvantages. For one thing, it is expensive. Maintenance doses for transplant patients cost anywhere from $6,000 to $10,000 per year; while this cost may be reduced somewhat in the future, it will remain high. More important, however, are the drug's severe side effects. The major toxic effect of cyclosporine is impaired kidney function in virtually all patients who have used it (Strom and Loertscher, 1984:728). It has also been linked to liver damage, hypertension, and an increased risk of the cancer lymphoma (Austen and Cosimi, 1984:1437). Considerable research is underway to determine what combination of cyclosporine therapy and conventional immunosuppression will reduce the risk of such damage. Also, development of new forms of cyclosporine with comparable potency but less toxicity is expected in the future. In the meantime, though, the difficult question is whether or not the benefit of cyclosporine outweighs the risks, particularly in hastening the onset of kidney failure. In a bitter irony, this drug is eventually destroying the very organ it saved.

Unanswered Questions in Organ Transplantation

In addition to the issues surrounding cyclosporine, organ transplantation raises many other serious policy questions. One prominent problem concerns guaranteeing a sufficient supply of organs, especially those (such as the heart, pancreas, and liver) that require a brain-dead donor. Austen and Cosimi (1984:1437) estimated that the number of suitable heart donors was about 2,000. Although this pool is satisfactory now, if the use of heart transplants widens substantially, a major donor shortage is anticipated.

The donor problem is complicated by the fact that the families of many suitable donors do not give permission. The just-mentioned figure of 2,000 represents only 10 to 15 percent of the people who suffer brain death each year and could serve as organ donors, but the Uniform Act for the Donation of Organs requires the documentation of consent before organs can be transplanted. Although the rate of donations may rise through education campaigns, the overall size of the pool might actually shrink as medicine learns to save more of these people (Wehr, 1984:458). Government is understandably hesitant to intervene and fund procurement of organs from unwilling or even uncertain donors.

Could the organ-donation act be amended to presume consent in the absence of any documents to the contrary? Mark Cwiek (1984:99) states boldly, "The solution seems clear: action must be taken now to promote the availability of needed human organs and to avoid creating greater social and moral problems. The passage of presumed consent laws in all of these fifty states must become a priority of the highest order." Although this approach, currently used in Belgium, might resolve the supply problem, it contradicts our basic values concerning personal autonomy. According to Engelhardt (1984:70), "the more one presumes that organs are not societal property, the more difficult it is to justify shifting the burden to individuals to show they do not want their organs used." Although Engelhardt agrees that it is unfortunate if potential recipients die because insufficient organs are available for transplantation, he says it is not unfair, because other values (e.g., keeping the body intact for burial) must be protected in a free society. "Free societies," he concludes (1984:70–71), "are characterized by the commitment to live with tragedies that result from the decisions of free individuals not to participate in the beneficent endeavors of others."

Another scarcity, reaching crisis proportions much faster, centers on the blood supply. On the one hand, the donor pool has contracted, in part due to the public's fear of AIDS. On the other hand, the demand for blood continues to escalate as more surgeries and organ transplants—some of which require over 100 units of blood—are performed. Alfred Grindon, director of the American Red Cross Blood Services in Atlanta, predicts that fewer units of blood will be available in the future (Bosy, 1987:2). He expects ethical dilemmas over access to blood, as those with money or connections seek to use their influence to gain priority over those who cannot make special arrangements. This scarcity of blood also raises questions as to whether surgeries that place extraordinary strains on the blood supply can continue to take precedence.

On the broader level of policy making, organ transplants provide another clear example of the conflict between the prevailing view in our culture, that no expense should be spared to save an individual's life and the reality that the gigantic costs of such extreme measures might preclude more productive uses of limited health-care resources. Albert Jonsen (1986:10), for instance, argues that the artificial heart threatens to deprive many persons of access to needed medical care:

> The threat appears first in the likelihood that public expenditures will be drawn to this technology, rather than toward preventive measures that would have, overall, a more beneficial effect on health . . . the added burden on publicly financed health care will force certain budgetary reallocations. These are likely to affect less visible, less "urgent" expenses such as those for health education, screening, prevention, community clinics, hospital stay, and so forth.

Arnold Relman, editor of the *New England Journal of Medicine,* suggests further that the emphasis on organ transplants threatens to divert money from pressing social needs such as housing, education and the environment (Rodgers, 1984:63). Despite these concerns, though, Schroeder and Hunt (1987:3145) undoubtedly are correct when they conclude that "cardiac transplantation is clearly here to stay as a valid therapeutic option."

Organ transplants, like all expensive life-saving treatments, raise innumerable questions of social priorities. Do they represent the efficient use of health-care resources? Do they justify the tradeoffs required to provide the requisite amount of resources? Does the state have authority to redistribute financial resources—or the organs themselves—so as to enable transplant surgery for all those who would benefit? Finally, in a liberal society does a dying person have a right to a new organ? How far does this right extend when it conflicts with the rights of others to more basic health-care needs? These difficult questions of fairness, equity, efficiency, and cost are inescapable.

In spite of all the technical advances, it is still unclear how many lives are usefully extended by new organs. Even under optimal circumstances, 30 to 40 percent of liver transplants will fail within a month, and during that month the patient endures considerable pain, both physically and emotionally. Even if the patient survives for a year or two or more, post-transplant existence is often excruciating for the patient and family. Hale (1984) describes the post-surgical ordeals of patients who have undergone transplant surgery and must now live "tethered to medical treatment for life." She cites the high suicide rates among kidney transplant patients, as well as less extreme forms of revolt against the loss of control over their lives following the surgery.

In our quest to prolong life at all costs, we may again be losing sight of quality-of-life concerns. As Kenneth Vaux has said, "we are going to have to temper our ambitions and learn to accept the inevitability of the disease, the inevitability of death itself" (Friedrich, 1984:75). We must learn that not everything that can be done to prolong a life must be done if the quality of that life is distinctly subhuman. We must first distinguish those cases where life is meaningfully extended from those in which the benefit to the person is marginal at best. And we must keep in mind the tradeoffs implicit in any large single investment such as an organ transplant.

Government Involvement in Transplantation

By 1972, kidney dialysis had improved dramatically and demand far outstripped supply, thus necessitating a private rationing system. In passing the End Stage Renal Disease (ESRD) program that year, Congress took the easy way out. Giving in to the proponents, public-relations campaign which included putting a kidney patient on dialysis during a Ways and Means Committee hearing, Congress extended Medicare coverage to all kidney patients—at the same time as it increased taxes to bail out Medicare, which already faced imminent bankruptcy. Eighty percent of kidney dialysis and transplant costs are now borne by the federal government.

The ESRD program is often cited as a case in disastrous medical policy making. Because original estimates severely underestimated the number of eligible patients, the first-year costs of $241 million far exceeded the estimate of $135 million. By 1983, the cost of the ESRD program exceeded $2 billion per year for approximately 70,000 patients. As a result these patients, who represent about 0.25 percent of all Medicare beneficiaries, account for 13 percent of total Medicare expenditures for out-patient care and almost 10 percent of all Medicare B (in-patient) costs. The advent of federal funding made the dialysis population not only considerably larger, but also sicker and older. In 1967, only 7 percent of dialysis patients were over 55; by 1983, the percentage had climbed to 45. Many U.S. dialysis patients suffer from other diseases that would exclude them from treatment in Britain and other countries that have a national health service.

According to Robert Rubin, a kidney specialist and HHS Assistant Secretary for Planning and Evaluation, any sort of transplant entitlement program can force the government to pour money into patients with little chance of survival: "You might not want to transplant someone with cancer beyond the margins of the liver but if it's a federal program, heck, you do it" (Wehr, 1984:458). As Annas (1985:187) notes, however, the ESRD decision "simply served to postpone the time when identical decisions will have to be made about candidates for heart and liver transplantation." That time has now arrived, and the ESRD experience makes Congress unlikely to rush into support for federal funding of liver and heart transplants.

On the other hand, policy makers face significant political pressures to guarantee access to new organs to those who need it. Just as the ESRD program was the result of emotional lobbying efforts, so today office holders increasingly are becoming the targets of constituents who appeal for public aid in obtaining and paying for expensive transplant surgeries. Most difficult to resist are the pleas for lifesaving transplants from the parents of young children. Speaker of the House Tip O'Neill, CBS's Dan Rather, President Reagan, and many other notables have succumbed to these emotional pleas and interceded on behalf of particular patients who have made it into the public spotlight. At the local level as well, media publicity has often assisted the cause of patients or their parents.

In one well-publicized case, the parents of 11-month-old Jamie Fiske led a high-profile campaign in 1982 to obtain funding for her liver transplant. With the leverage of the local press and politicians, the Fiskes forced Blue Cross/Blue Shield to agree to pay for the surgery. Once successful at that stage, the Fiskes appeared at the national convention of the American Academy of Pediatrics to ask for a liver donor. The story hit the national news and Jamie had a new liver in eight days. Similarly, in 1983 the parents of Adriane Broderick got Congress to order the Military Medical Program to finance her transplant. White House aide Michael Batten reportedly estimated that his activities in pressuring private health insurers and state Medicaid directors to finance liver transplants have "forced 20 states to pay for liver transplantations when they otherwise might have declined" (Wehr, 1984:455).

The power of public relations means that the distribution of organ transplants makes very little sense from a medical or ethical standpoint. In one case, for instance, a child judged to be a poor medical risk was given two transplants partly because congressional and media attention made the patient a cause célèbre (Rodgers, 1984:63). Parents who followed the formal procedures for obtaining a donor heart for their infant were outraged when publicity over the denial of a heart transplant for "Baby Jesse" resulted in immediate access to a heart transplant for Jesse over those who had waited patiently. For every person who obtains a transplant through these methods, scores of others who might be better medical risks may die awaiting their turn.

Until recently, third-party payers have avoided reimbursing the cost of liver transplants on the basis that they represent experimental, not therapeutic procedures. Only those procedures shown to be reasonable and necessary therapeutic measures generally qualify for reimbursement. In 1983, however, a National Institutes of Health panel proclaimed liver transplants therapeutic, thus opening the way for a flood of potential transplant patients. "Armed with NIH's blessing, transplant boosters began demanding more operations, tried prying funds from reluctant insurers and pressed Congress and the Reagan Administration for Medicare coverage. Governors and legislators hurried aboard the transplant bandwagon" (Rodgers, 1984:62). Third-party payers' hopes of escaping the enormous costs appear doomed.

In response to the growing dispute over liver transplants, Congress passed a bill (S 2048, October 4, 1984) designed to ease the difficulties of patients and their families in seeking organ-transplant surgery and take these decisions out of the realm of public relations. Interestingly, a provision that would have financed cyclosporine for patients who could not afford the drug was omitted in the final version. The act (PL 98-507) authorized the expenditure of $2 million annually to support a national computerized system for matching patients with donors of these scarce organs. The proliferation of transplant centers across the country and the existence of more than 120 organ-retrieval agencies had made this need especially critical. Moreover, because of reports of many organs wasted for lack of skilled teams to save and transplant them, Congress authorized from $5 million in fiscal 1985 to $12 million in 1987 for grants to create or upgrade local and regional agencies that procure human organs for transplantation and that participate in the computerized matching network. The act also provided for a national registry of transplant patients to facilitate scientific evaluations of transplant procedures and directed the Secretary of Health and Human Services to assign responsibility for administering organ-transplant programs to the Public Health Service or another appropriate body. Finally, it prohibited the purchase or sale of human organs for transplantation and authorized jail terms of up to five years for deliberate violations of this provision. This last clause will gain significance as the proliferation of transplant centers produces a demand for suitable organs that outstrips the limited supply. It also demonstrates the government's claim to a compelling state interest in protecting individuals from economic pressures that would lead them to sell their organs.

Although this Organ Transplant Act is far from a repeat of the ESRD program, Congress still is largely unable to escape the growing pressures from constituents, interest groups, and the media to fund an expanding array of organ transplants.

The Organ Transplant Act also created a task force to study and report on the ethical, legal, and financial aspects of organ transplants. In July 1986, the National Task Force on Organ Transplantation issued its final report. Among its many recommendations, it called for federal financing of heart and liver transplants. In order to provide equitable access to these "gifts of life," the task force recommended that patient selection for transplantation be based on "publicly stated and fairly applied" medical criteria, including the need and the probability of success. It also recommended that the government should provide immunosuppressive medication to all patients who cannot afford it.

Furthermore, the task force recommended creation of a national network to coordinate all organ recovery and distribution. In order to ensure an adequate supply of organs to meet the increased demands government funding would unleash, the task force urged all states to enact the Uniform Definition of Death Act and Congress to adopt "routine inquiry/required request" legislation. The former action would make brain-dead bodies available for transplantation, while the latter would require hospitals to routinely ask all potential donors (or next of kin) if they wish to donate their organs.

Just before the task force issued its final report, HHS Secretary Otis Bowen announced the government's decision to start funding heart transplants for qualified Medicare patients. Under this action, heart transplant programs approved by the Health Care Financing Administration (HCFA) would be reimbursed. The criteria specify that, to be approved, a facility must have performed 12 or more heart transplants in each of the previous two years and 12 transplants before that. It must also have an average survival rate of at least 73 percent. As of November 1987, 11 transplant centers had qualified. Despite HHS projections of a maximum of 10 centers, this number is expected to increase.

In separate actions since 1986, the government has moved toward funding cyclosporine for all transplant patients and has established a national policy of required request for potential organ donors. Under the fiscal 1987 budget legislation (PL 99-509), hospitals that fail to establish required-request procedures would lose eligibility for participation in Medicare and Medicaid programs. Also, HHS has allocated over $5 million in grants for organ-procurement programs to coordinate recovery and distribution. Both of these actions have been taken to drastically increase the supply of organs, which, in view of the rapid movement toward governmental sanctioning and public funding of organ transplants, is the only factor holding back transplant programs. These steps by the government will accelerate the number of heart and liver transplants performed, much as occurred with kidney transplants in the 1970s. As in the case of treatment of severely ill newborns, the current response of policy makers to transplantation demonstrates the powerful momentum behind high-cost technological intervention in the United States.

Behavior Control and Modification

As we come to know more about the brain and its functioning we are, concurrently, overawed by its complexity yet confident that ultimately its deepest secrets will be unfolded, thus giving us the capacity to intervene in ways until recently the realm of science fiction. These emerging capabilities, promising us considerable control over the brain, may help us overcome a wide range of mental disabilities and behavioral problems. On the other hand, however, especially in dealing with behavior problems, the concept of regulating individual minds through direct intervention in the brain raises severe ethical and policy questions. Like genetic technology, recent innovations in brain intervention strike at the heart of our most basic notions of the human condition and challenge social values concerning personal autonomy and constitutional freedoms. They clearly raise the specter of social control and an Orwellian society.

Much of the popular literature has oversimplified and exaggerated the (admittedly rapid) advances in brain science and technology thus heightening the fears of those persons who see behavior control as a threat and creating unreasonable hope in those who might benefit. These interventions do not elicit specific and predictable behaviors; rather, they act upon the emotional state of the patient. Moreover, since no two human brains are alike, there is a large variation in effect from one person to the next and even in the same person over time. Therefore, despite our growing knowledge base, considerable uncertainty accompanies the application of any attempt to modify behavior. Also, the brain is not neatly divided into discrete units conforming to categories of behavior, further limiting the predictability of the effects of a particular intervention.

The methods of behavior control and modification include direct brain-intervention techniques such as electrical stimulation, psychosurgery, and psychotropic or mind-altering drugs. For each technique there are three application settings. The first is a voluntary patient who understands the potential risks and benefits of the procedure. It is not always clear, though, when a patient has given informed consent and procedural safeguards have been provided to distinguish free choice from the second type of application—on a patient who consents under duress. Institutionalized patients are particularly vulnerable to strong pressure to "consent" to procedures, including electroshock and surgery. The third and most problematic type of application is on a non-consenting patient—either one who is incompetent to decide rationally or one forced against his or her will to undergo the treatment. The line between therapy and experimentation can become blurred in all three applications, but the risk of solely experimental applications is highest in the third setting. After a brief review of brain intervention techniques, the policy issues are analyzed.

Direct Brain Intervention

Anyone who has seen the movie "One Flew Over the Cuckoo's Nest" will recall the electroshock (EST) scenes in which the patient is secured and a series of 70- to 150-volt shocks are administered to the nervous system, resulting in violent convulsions. Although electroshock treatment is now considered a very crude form of therapy, in the recent past it was a widely used form of behavior control—even the threat of EST was enough to pacify many institutionalized patients. EST can have beneficial effects on some patients, especially the severely depressed, and was the method of choice for many psychiatrists until alternative treatment approaches became available. Not surprisingly, despite its potential benefit for selected patients, EST was often used for control, not therapy, thus evoking widespread opposition to its use. Its violent image and its potential for abuse make EST difficult to justify as a therapy.

Electronic brain stimulation (ESB) has replaced EST as the most popular electronic means to ameliorate behavioral disorders. ESB induces not a permanent beneficial change but, instead, an emotional tranquility. It also can effectively relieve the psychological pain caused by severe anxiety and depression, replacing it with a feeling of euphoria. ESB uses thin, insulated wires, implanted in the brain, that allow electronic messages to be sent and recordings to be made from areas deep inside the brain. ESB has also been used successfully to treat epilepsy, intractable pain, violent aggressiveness, and chronic insomnia.

When used to treat abnormal aggressiveness, ESB treatment must be repeated periodically. Once the electrodes are implanted, brain activity can be monitored and warning signs of an impending crisis identified. This diagnostic capacity might be the only means of revealing abnormal patterns of electrical activity deep inside the brain. The development of miniaturized electronic devices—stimoceivers—permits instantaneous radio transmission to and from the brains of subjects. Computers enable remote monitoring of brain activities—and also allow considerable control over the subject's brain, thereby raising severe ethical questions. For instance, some observers (Ingraham and Smith, 1972) have suggested the use of such devices on prison parolees to monitor their activities, movements, and brain waves by computers in centralized locations (much like an air traffic control system). The opposition to this proposal has been intense. ESB, however, clearly demonstrates that even a technique of unquestioned medical value can also have tremendous potential for abuse. By allowing such extensive control of a person's general mood, ESB arouses basic concerns of personal autonomy and self-determination.

The most controversial type of physical brain intervention, because it results in permanent destruction of particular regions of the brain, is psychosurgery. Brain surgery, when used to repair physical damage caused by head injuries or tumors, is a credible and accepted therapeutic procedure (known as neurosurgery). When the same techniques are used instead to correct mental or behavioral disorders (psychosurgery), they become highly controversial. These applications rest on the assumption that behavioral disorders have an organic base and must be corrected by physical intervention, not psychotherapy. Chorover (1981) and other critics of psychosurgery have forcefully questioned this assumption. Furthermore, the short history of psychosurgery does not inspire confidence.

According to Valenstein (1986:3), between 1948 and 1952 "tens of thousands of mutilating brain operations were performed on mentally ill men and women," including many from the United States who "voluntarily" underwent lobotomy. Although the practice of lobotomy was curtailed by 1960, primarily because of the availability of psychoactive drugs as an inexpensive alternative, in its wake it left many seriously brain-damaged persons.

Frontal lobotomies entail cutting the frontal lobes off from the rest of the brain, thereby making them inoperable. Although several techniques were used to lobotomize approximately 70,000 persons in the late 1940s and early 1950s, Walter Freeman achieved particular notoriety for his use of transorbital lobotomy. Freeman casually summarized the technique in its gruesome details:

> I have also been trying out a sort of half-way stage between electroshock and prefrontal lobotomy on some of the patients. This consists of knocking them out with a shock and while they are under the "anesthetic" thrusting an ice pick up between the eyeball and the eyelid through the roof of the orbit actually into the frontal lobe of the brain and making the lateral cut by swinging the thing from side to side. I have done two patients on both sides and another on one side without running into any complications, except a very black eye in one case. There may be trouble later on but it seemed fairly easy, although definitely a disagreeable thing to watch. It remains to be seen how these cases hold up, but so far they have shown considerable relief of their symptoms, and only some of the minor behavior difficulties that follow lobotomy. They can even get up and go home within an hour or so (Valenstein, 1986:203).

The term "ice-pick surgery" is literally accurate. Although Freeman eventually developed the "transorbital leucotome" and then the "orbitoclast" as the instruments designed to withstand the tremendous pressures necessary to crush through the orbit before severing the brain, the first transorbital lobotomy in his office was performed using a tool with the name "Uline Ice Co." on its handle (Valenstein, 1986:202).

Many recipients of lobotomies were indigent patients in state hospitals, but a substantial number were well-to-do women in private hospitals and physicians' offices. The transorbital procedure left only small scars on the eyelids and could be performed in a matter of minutes. To some extent, frontal lobotomies took on a fad-like image. The fact that such a gruesome and intrusive technique won not only uncritical acceptance by the medical profession as a whole (despite a few vocal detractors) but also widespread public approval and mass-media support as a miracle cure again illustrates our society's faith in technological fixes. This dependence was easily transferred to the less dramatic approach of psychoactive drug therapy after 1960.

The demise of lobotomies did not end psychosurgery. Sophisticated tools known as stereotaxic instruments have facilitated more precise placement of electrodes on specific brain targets thus allowing for the destruction of relatively small areas of brain tissue. Electrolytic lesioning or selective cutting of nerve fibers is conducted after the region to be lesioned is localized by establishing coordinates using anatomical landmarks and X-rays.

> Through small holes drilled into the patient's skull, the surgeon inserts a dye permitting location of the target structures with X-ray photography. The photographs are then used to calibrate the stereotaxic instrument. Transferred to the patient's head, the instrument and micromanipulators are positioned and electrodes inserted through openings in the skull. If the patient's response to electric current passed through the electrodes indicates that the electrodes are positioned correctly, a stronger current is sent through the wire to produce small lesions or coagulations (Delgado, 1982:147).

Radiation, cryoprobes (freezing), or focused ultrasonic beams have also been used to destroy the tissue.

As with lobotomies, however, there is no way to predict the consequences of these procedures in either the short or long run. Chorover (1981:291), decrying psychosurgery as a highly experimental procedure that "produces a marked deterioration in behavior, serious impairments of judgment, and other disastrous social adjustment effects," has called for a temporary moratorium on psychosurgery and for more basic research on brain mechanisms and behavior. In contrast, Valenstein (1986:285) contends that after a lag in psychosurgery since the mid-1970s, new knowledge about the brain, combined with the development of better surgical techniques, seems to have justified reconsideration of psychosurgery for patients who do not respond to other treatment. Although the National Commission for the Protection of Human Subjects (1975) criticized the use of psychosurgery for social or institutional control, it concluded that, as currently practiced, it might help some patients. It recommended prior screening of each proposed surgery by an independent institutional review board (IRB), but its recommendations never translated into federal legislation or regulations. Instead, action restricting psychosurgery has originated in state legislatures. Oregon, for instance, in 1982 passed a statute prohibiting psychosurgery, and California's stringent regulations have all but ended the practice in that state. Although most states have not taken action, primarily because of the threat of liability, fewer than 200 psychosurgeries are performed annually in the United States.

Ironically, concurrent with the imposition of legal restraints, extensions of studies originally reported to the National Commission have been favorable to psychosurgery for certain classes of patients. Two independent research teams (Teuber, Corkin, and Twitchell, 1977; Mirsky and Orzack, 1977) reported that psychosurgery significantly improved quality of life for between 70 and 80 percent of patients. Furthermore, they found no evidence of physical, emotional, or intellectual impairment caused by the surgery.

Careful patient selection and use only as a last resort for those patients who fail to respond to drug therapy seem central criteria for any future uses of psychosurgery. In any other situations, psychosurgery engenders significant debate. In 1970 Vernon Mark and Frank Ervin, in their book *Violence and the Brain,* charged that much of the violence in the U.S. is caused by brain pathology. According to Mark and Erwin, patients with "discontrol syndrome" were prone to sudden violent outbursts triggered by abnormal electrical discharges in the temporal lobe. The authors recommended an ambitious effort to locate the triggers of these outbursts and remove them. This call for preventive brain surgery as a means of dealing with a social problem raised directly the question of social control of behavior judged troublesome or abnormal and unleashed intense controversy.

Thomas Szasz (1974) champions the opposite viewpoint. He contends that diagnostic labels in psychiatry are myths used to stigmatize social deviants. With its use of involuntary confinement, mind-altering drugs, and psychosurgery, Szasz asserts, psychiatry has become a political force, concealing social conflict by calling it illness or justifying coercion as treatment. Chorover (1981:291) agrees that although psychosurgery has unique characteristics, in terms of social policy it is merely one of a large number of "psychotechnological" means of dealing with individuals or groups vaguely defined as aggressive, disruptive, dangerous, or uncooperative. "Insofar as the causes of social conflict actually lie in the domain of social affairs, psychotechnological treatment of deviants should be regarded as a perversion of medicine and a distinct threat to individual liberty"

(Chorover, 1981:291). Chorover agrees that we must assess the impact and social consequences of psychotechnology within the broad context of politics and public policy, or else we will surrender both our constitutional freedom and our human dignity.

Psychosurgery, then, will continue to generate policy issues on a range of levels. First is the dilemma of consent. Because the consent must come from the damaged organ itself, if the damage is severe enough to warrant surgery who can give consent for an irreversible procedure? Second is the interplay of therapy and experimentation: because each brain is unique, psychosurgery will always have a high degree of uncertainty and thus risk. Third is the debatable assumption that deviant behavior has an organic base. If it does not, can we justify the use of organic procedures such as surgery to resolve a nonorganic problem? Are we not simply treating the symptoms without attacking the cause?

Psychosurgery also vividly illustrates problems of social control. We are developing an impressive array of techniques to control or modify behavior. Each technique, however, offers tremendous opportunity for abuse and poses serious threats to individual liberty. Stigmatization of those labeled abnormal, unethical constraints on freedom of choice, and erosion of individual dignity seem almost inseparable from psychosurgery. Yet, there is evidence that psychosurgery and ESB are beneficial to many individuals and represent some person's only hope of leading a near-normal existence. To deny them the benefits of these technologies because we do not trust our ability to set reasonable limits on their use seems unfair.

Controlling Behavior through Drugs

Many of the same issues raised by physical brain intervention also arise in chemical intervention. Though not as irreversible as psychosurgery, the use of drugs to produce desired moods and mental functioning and thus influence behavior poses parallel policy questions and makes similar assumptions regarding the organic base of behavior problems. Chemical control is a considerably more urgent issue, though, because it enjoys such widespread and socially accepted usage. The ease of administration and the potential for surreptitious application make this form of control more threatening than physical methods.

Three major groups of psychotropic drugs are used as therapeutic agents. The first and most powerful is the antipsychotic drugs or major tranquilizers. FDA approval of chlorpromazine (Thorazine) in 1954 initiated the use of this group of drugs in the treatment of major mental illnesses such as schizophrenia and paranoia. These drugs have sedative, hypnotic, and mood-elevating effects. Although they do nothing to cure, but rather suppress the symptoms of the disease, they are effective in maintaining emotional equilibrium for many patients. Maintenance therapy requires prolonged use, generally at reduced dose levels. Discontinuance of the drug will result in return of symptoms. The major tranquilizers have also been used in treating violence. Administration of these drugs, however, is complex because effects and dosage levels vary across individuals and prolonged use can have deleterious side effects.

The second major group of psychotropic drugs is the antidepressants, including amphetamines, Ritalin, Preludin, monoamine oxidose inhibitors, and tricyclic derivatives of imipramine. Although amphetamines have little clinical value in treating depression because of their very short duration, they are widely known and used. They also have considerable potential for abuse and dependency. Ritalin is a stimulant that has been found to have an opposite (calming) effect on hyperactive children, thus leading to its overuse in some school districts. The use of drugs in schools for social control has come under considerable, deserved attack in recent decades because the effects of prolonged exposure are unknown. Ritalin has, in fact, been linked to complex changes in the central nervous system, and questions concerning its impact on personality development, innovative thinking capacity, and psychological or physiological dependence remain unanswered.

The third group of psychoactive drugs is the antianxiety drugs or minor tranquilizers. These include barbiturates, which are the least effective and have a high tendency to produce dependence, habituation, and addiction. Despite these factors and their low margin of safety, barbiturates such as phenobarbital are effective in treating epilepsy. Another group of minor tranquilizers include diazepoxides, such as Librium and Valium, which effectively control muscle spasms, hysteria in acute grief situations, and compulsion. They are less dangerous than barbiturates and less addictive. Minor tranquilizers, though not effective against psychoses, have special value in treatment of tension and anxiety associated with situational states and stress. The long-term use of antianxiety drugs is discouraged, however, because they can produce dependence and are easily abused.

In addition to the psychotropic drugs, the use of hormonal treatment to control behavior has proceeded rapidly since the 1970s. Studies have repeatedly found connections between aggression and testosterone, and elevated levels of this male hormone have been implicated in sex-related violent crimes. The administration of female hormones to control aggressive males has been successful in treating abnormal sexual preoccupation. The hormone Depro-Provera has also been used to inhibit the male sex drive. In large doses Depro-Provera serves, in effect, as a chemical castration by shrinking the testes.

Increasingly drugs are used to alter behavior, not because of a compelling scientific consensus as to how they help patients, but because they are effective and convenient. In other words, biomedical technology is being used for non-medical reasons in order to accomplish other policy objectives. In a rights-oriented society, this practice should raise serious constitutional questions. However, ours has also become a drug-oriented society, in which psychoactive drugs are routinely accepted coping mechanisms for day-to-day problems. To a large extent, drugs have become a quick fix for the anxiety, depression, and social stresses of modern-day existence. In such a context, opposition to therapeutic use of drugs by normal, let alone seriously ill, persons is an unpopular stance.

Human Experimentation

The ethical concerns and policy issues associated with human medical experimentation largely arose from the horrors of Nazi Germany. The war-crimes trials, revealing the genocide of entire populations and the German medical research community's compliance in inhumane experiments, gave birth to worldwide demands for a code of experimental ethics. The Nuremberg trials uncovered the stunning fact that large numbers of concentration-camp prisoners were used for purposes of medical experimentation. Still more shocking, many of the researchers were persons of international reputation. Their arguments that the acquisition of knowledge and advancement of social ends justified the means demonstrated the need for a codified ethical framework for human experimentation.

After the Nuremberg trials, the judicial tribunal, with help from expert physicians drafted the Nuremberg Code, a landmark effort in specifying the relationship between medical experimenter and subject. This lengthy document contains ten propositions, which can be summarized as follows:

1. The voluntary consent of the human subject is absolutely essential.

2. The experiment should yield fruitful results for the good of society unobtainable by other methods or means of study.

3. The experiment should be designed and based on the results of previously conducted animal experimentation.

4. The experiment should be designed to avoid all unnecessary physical and mental suffering and injury.

5. No experiment should be conducted where there is an a priori reason to believe that death or disabling injury will occur.

6. The degree of risk should never exceed the determined humanitarian importance of the problems under investigation.

7. Adequate preparation is required to protect the experimental subject against even remote possibilities of injury, death, or disability.

8. The experiment should be conducted only by scientifically qualified persons.

9. During the course of an experiment, human subjects should be at liberty to bring the experiment to an end.

10. During the course of an experiment, the scientist in charge must be prepared to terminate the experiment at any stage if in his judgment continuation of the experiment is likely to result in injury, disability, or death to the experimental subjects.

The Code emphasizes proper disclosure, voluntary consent of the human subject, and especially the basic traditional safeguard so long practiced between the physician and his patient: first of all, do not cause injury. Just as the individual patient's welfare must be of foremost importance in the physician-patient relationship, so the first responsibility of the researcher is to the human experimental subject.

The Nuremberg Code was followed by many more specific or expansive codes. The World Medical Association's "Declaration of Helsinki" reiterated major provisions of the Nuremberg Code, as did the American Medical Association's "Principles of Medical Ethics," established in 1971. Most other medical associations worldwide have adopted codes of ethical standards incorporating the theme that the patient's interest is of paramount importance.

Nevertheless, violations of ethical principles did not end with the Nazi experimenters. Unfortunately, the tremendous expansion of expenditures for medical research after World War II and the intensified search for medical knowledge, along with researchers' heightened personal concern for being the first to make new discoveries, led to unethical research on human subjects in the United States—not brought to light until the startling revelations of the 1960s and 1970s. Children at the Willowbrook State Hospital on Staten Island, New York, for instance, were deliberately infected with viral hepatitis. Likewise, the Jewish Chronic Diseases Hospital in Brooklyn, New York, injected cancer cells into senile patients without their knowledge for experimental, not therapeutic, purposes. The most shocking of the many (documented by Katz, 1972) ethical violations was the Tuskegee, Alabama, syphilis study in which 300 rural black males with diagnosed syphilis were left untreated so that the natural course of the disease could be documented, even after antibiotics were available to cure it. The discovery that the U.S. government authorized and funded this research for almost four decades led to widespread media coverage and a public outcry.

The original U.S. Public Health Service regulations for research were revised and strengthened considerably in 1974. Public law 93–348 mandated the use of local institutional review boards (IRBs) to review biomedical and behavioral research involving human subjects. All institutions involved in federally funded research had to establish an IRB under this act, although the specifics of IRBs still vary considerably. The 1974 legislation also called for the creation of a national commission to study the ethical aspects of human experimentation. The National Commission for the Protection of Human Subjects of Biomedical and Behavioral Research spent four years investigating, debating, and analyzing a range of topics, including informed consent; selection of research subjects; the use of fetuses, children, prisoners, and the mentally infirm as research subjects; psychosurgery; and sterilization.

In 1978 the National Commission published a report that served as the basis for another revision of federal legislation. After extensive public response to the new proposals, the revised regulations were published in the *Federal Register* in June 1981. The IRB format was clarified and extended. IRBs are now common in hospitals and medical centers, representing visible evidence of a commitment to protect patients from potential abuse.

The IRB regulations must be distinguished from the suggestions by the President's Commission on biomedical ethics, in 1983 that health-care institutions experiment with ethics committees to help make life-death decisions concerning treatment of specific patients. According to Fost and Crawford (1985:2691), "Hospital ethics committees are increasingly becoming part of decision making involving life support in critically ill patients." The bureaucratization of medicine through these ethics committees has received harsh criticism: "The use of institutional ethics committees (IECs) is, unfortunately, the sign of the times. Their development symbolizes the dreary, depressed, and disorganized state to which American medicine has fallen. Not only have physicians lost political and economic power; they have also lost the autonomy to reach medical decisions" (Siegler, 1986:22). IECs should not be confused, however, with IRBs evaluating medical research.

Although IRBs are commonplace (Greenwald, Ryan and Mulvihill, 1982:xii), no two of them have been implemented in the same way. There is little uniformity of procedure, considerable variation in standards for acceptable consent forms, and wide variance in their composition and in the proportion of public (non-hospital) members. A survey of 61 IRBs by Gray, Cooke and Tannenbaum (1978) prior to the latest regulations revealed that many were deficient in their responsibilities and lacked impact on the consent process. Questions persist, despite two decades of experience, in the areas of consent, acceptable benefit-risk criteria, and compliance.

Despite these problems, the use of human subjects in medical experimentation is not optional. No matter how much testing is conducted on laboratory animals (itself a highly controversial subject among animal-rights groups), ultimately the tests must be conducted on humans. There is no way to extrapolate fully from animal models to humans even when the animal model is appropriate, and in some instances, such as species-specific infections, animal experimentation is not relevant at all. Therefore, if we are to have any progress in overcoming disease, we will continue to require large numbers of human subjects for a variety of experiments.

Nor can one argue naively for full disclosure of all experiments to the subjects, for this is contrary to controlled-experiment design. Under a double-blind protocol, the control group is given a placebo (the sugar pill) and even the experimenter cannot know who is getting the treatment or drug being tested. Strict secrecy is essential in order to eliminate bias. While subjects must be protected from exploitation or unacceptable risk, destroying the scientific integrity of the experiment would make it useless. Although IRBs and other formal arrangements minimize abuse of subjects, there is a considerable gray area where problems will continue to exist regarding informed consent. But the fact that we can never fully resolve this dilemma of consent should not discourage continued efforts to guarantee full protection of subjects.

Another problem that continues to haunt human medical experimentation is its alleged social bias. According to Kieffer (1975:124), this is a particular problem since it is the poor, uneducated, or functionally illiterate who "comprise 80 percent of the human subjects used in experimentation." To some extent this predominance of the socially deprived has been alleviated by proscribing experimentation in prisons and state institutions, where these social groups are overrepresented. Nevertheless, economic factors reinforce the bias, since treatment in experimental situations is usually free. The well-to-do or those with adequate insurance are less vulnerable to such pressures. In contrast, an indigent sick person is likely to take a considerably higher risk that is offered without cost. Or, if one's child has a rare disease and private hospitalization is out of the question, an experimental treatment may represent the only hope, even if it is made clear to the parents that it is an experiment. The frequent shift from volunteers to paid subjects only heightens the potential for economic exploitation.

Likewise, most drug testing (especially the most risky Phase I, which tests safety in human administration) has used subjects who are willing to take the risk with little promise of benefit. This practice raises critical policy questions concerning the distribution of risks and benefits in society, because it is likely that most of the benefits accrued will go to those who can afford the treatment if it proves safe and effective through clinical trials. Ironically, public policies designed to protect vulnerable U.S. citizens (such as prisoners and other institutionalized persons) has largely shifted the most risky experimentation to the poor in other countries. This move simply recasts the sensitive questions of exploitation because it is even more unlikely that these new subjects will benefit from the successful research efforts.

Medical research is most questionable when patients may or may not benefit from the experimental treatment. In such cases, patients generally are unlikely to question the judgment of a physician in whose trust they have voluntarily placed themselves. This inherently unequal physician-patient relationship puts undue pressure on the patient to participate even when the hope for a cure is remote. The patient might fear that refusal to participate will be interpreted as a denial of the physician's wisdom.

These touchy situations require a mechanism providing independent second opinions for patients who are admitted to experimental programs. Where the physician has a financial or professional stake in recruiting patients to participate in drug or treatment trials, special precautions are necessary. Says Robert Levine (quoted in Budiansky, 1987:58), "There have been allegations that in some clinical trials there are great pressures to recruit enough patients or they'll lose their funding. In these circumstances, they might be tempted to paint a rosier picture."

Recently, another dimension of the experimental dilemma has surfaced as desperately ill patients, particularly those with cancer or AIDS, have criticized the slowness of drug trials and demanded access to drugs they feel might help them. For instance, when clinical trials found that the drug AZT relieved symptoms in some AIDS cases, other AIDS patients adamantly demanded that the trials be cut short and the drug made available. In other words, they insisted on their right to be, in effect, experimental subjects. For AIDS patients, however, there simply are no better alternatives at present. In June 1987 a new federal regulation permitted drug companies to sell promising yet still experimental drugs to terminally ill patients (*Medical World News,* 1987). By short-circuiting traditional experimental protocol, this regulation sets a dangerous precedent.

5 Death Related Issues in Biomedicine

The tremendous advances in technology's capacity to keep the human body biologically alive have also, ironically, deepened some people's commitment to defend the patient's right to die. As mechanical respirators, artificial organs, and invasive life-prolonging treatments permit the almost indefinite extension of biological existence, the medical profession is questioning of the ethic of keeping the patient alive at all costs. Increasingly, the use of artificial support systems is quietly rejected, particularly among chronically ill elderly patients. DNR (do not resuscitate) instructions or "no codes," often unwritten, limiting the use of livesaving treatment are commonplace in hospitals. The general public is displaying a similar disillusion with high-technology life extension. The desire to die with dignity, free from the tubes and machines, reflects a growing disenchantment with technological prolongation of life and raises demands for euthanasia policies.

What role should the government take in decisions to forego life-sustaining treatment? The President's Commission (1983:1) argued that because death today is a much less private matter than it once was, usually occurring in a hospital or nursing home with many people involved, the "resolution of disagreements among them is more likely to require formal rules and means of adjudication." Furthermore, because biomedical developments have made death more a matter of deliberate decision, what once was the province of fate now becomes a matter of human choice. Although the commission's long report concluded that the major responsibility for ensuring "morally justified processes of decision making" lies with physicians, it called for institutional safeguards to protect the best interests of patients.

In addition to clarifying the rights, duties, and liabilities of all concerned parties, a process in which the courts and legislatures as well as legal and ethical commentators have become embroiled, the government has been drawn into several other highly sensitive death-related areas. The first of these, discussed in chapter 4, deals with government-mandated aggressive treatment for severely ill newborns. Baby Doe will not disappear as a critical policy issue. Second, the government, particularly at the state level, is involved in the reinvigorated debate over euthanasia in general. Many states have passed various types of legislation specifying the socially acceptable boundaries of euthanasia, particularly when it entails the withholding of artificial life-support systems. Third, the states are intimately involved in redefining death to correspond to the technological advances of the last decades. The swift movement from respiratory death to brain death as the generally accepted standard reflects both the new demand for transplant organs and the public awareness that life on machines is not always preferable to death.

Euthanasia

The dramatic expansion of the capacity to prolong life with an array of artificial support systems has raised severe ethical dilemmas concerning the circumstances under which available lifesaving treatment should be terminated. No single biomedical issue has more implications for public policy than euthanasia. Although considerable attention has been focused on euthanasia in terms of terminally ill elderly patients, the concept encompasses many death-hastening actions—withholding treatment from severely ill newborns, unplugging life-support machines at any age, or injecting fatal doses of pain-killing drugs into suffering patients, to name a few.

Although euthanasia is by no means new, recent advances in biomedical technology have complicated its meaning. Defined as "good death" by the

Greeks, it applied most clearly to "exposure" of sick newborns (Aristotle, *Politics,* 327) or to withholding of the limited medical interventions available for the elderly ill. The Greeks defined euthanasia in terms of the interest of the community more than the individual. According to Plato (*Republic,* 98), for instance, "if a man had a sickly constitution and intemperate habits, his life was worth nothing to himself or to anyone else; medicine was not meant for such people and they should not be treated, though they might be richer than Midas."

The present-day availability of extremely intensive (and expensive) interventions designed to extend the life of an individual increases the policy significance of such decisions, and most Americans have adopted an individual-rights approach to the value of life that Plato's utilitarian intuitions would not have allowed. As a result, the term euthanasia carries negative connotations and is often linked by its opponents with Nazi Germany and genocide. Colorado Governor Richard Lamm's suggestion, that elderly patients have a duty to younger generations to refuse certain kinds of treatment that would extend their lives at great expense, was roundly criticized by many interest groups, though it received surprisingly strong public support.

Classification of Types of Euthanasia

One reason why euthanasia elicits so much controversy is that it deals with death and with questions of who, if anyone, can make irrevocable decisions to die or let die. Few of us like to deal with the topic of death at all, let alone take responsibility for making a life-death decision. The multiple categories of euthanasia, each with an infinite range of permutations, add further complications and misunderstanding. Critics of euthanasia focus their arguments on the most threatening categories and cases, while supporters emphasize the least threatening types. For this reason it is important to begin by categorizing the applications of euthanasia (see table 2). Many classification schemes have been introduced in the literature, but they generally include two key dimensions. The first dimension, represented by either several discrete categories or a continuum, relates to the degree to which the patient has given or refused to give voluntary consent to the action. The second dimension concerns whether euthanasia is carried out in a passive or active form.

Voluntariness

Euthanasia is classified as "voluntary" if it is done with the patient's express consent—that is, if the patient has unambiguously expressed a desire to be either allowed or helped to die. Those opposed to all forms of euthanasia attack its voluntary form on several grounds. Some equate it with suicide and argue on sanctity-of-life grounds that society cannot condone such an act. According to these critics, a person has no right to die and

T A B L E   2
Catagories of euthanasia

	Passive (omission of measures to prolong life)	Active (direct inducement of death)
Voluntary with patient's express and informed consent	*Passive Voluntary* conscious, rational patient refuses life-prolonging treatment and request is granted	*Active Voluntary* conscious, rational patient requests and is given lethal injection
Speculative without patient's express and informed consent (e.g., comatose patient, infant, mentally retarded person)	*Passive Speculative* cessation of life-prolonging treatment for comatose patient or patient otherwise unable to give informed consent	*Active Speculative* lethal injection administered to comatose patient or patient otherwise unable to give informed consent
Involuntary against patient's express consent	*Passive Involuntary* cessation of life-prolonging treatment to conscious, rational person against his or her will	*Active Involuntary* lethal injection administered to conscious, rational patient against his or her will

must try to remain alive at all costs. There is always some chance of a miracle cure or remission. Anyone who wishes to end his or her life, it is argued, is irrational and should certainly not be encouraged or helped to carry out that desire.

Another, more practically oriented argument against voluntary euthanasia contends that many patients who express a will to die are acting under economic and social pressures or are in the temporary grip of depression or pain. In other words, the context is directing their will so that it is no longer free and unconstrained. For example, patients who feel they have become a burden to their family might convince themselves they really want to die. Although this possibility justifies caution in using euthanasia, it alone should not eliminate access to that choice for all patients. Voluntary euthanasia, though controversial, is the least problem-laden form.

At the other extreme is involuntary euthanasia, conducted over the patient's express opposition. This situation differs drastically from the previous one. Although some opponents of euthanasia argue that there is no difference between voluntary and involuntary applications (i.e., that it is wrong under any circumstances), most observers see voluntariness as a key variable and thus support voluntary decisions while rejecting involuntary euthanasia as akin to murder. Few commentators today are willing to permit involuntary applications within the realm of acceptability.

The most controversial and problematic cases are those which fall somewhere between these two ends of the voluntariness continuum. These involve persons who, for whatever reason, cannot give informed consent. Infants, children, and some mentally retarded patients are viewed as unable to consent to euthanasia because they lack the capacity to understand the implications of their decisions. Similarly, comatose patients are unable to communicate their desires at the time the decision must be made. These "speculative" instances are the most difficult because we simply do not know what the person would decide if given the opportunity.

Speculative euthanasia requires a proxy consent, usually by family or friends, similar to the consent given for any medical procedure. Critics of euthanasia reject this surrogate-consent option, arguing that it can easily lead to abuse or subordination of the patient's interest to that of the family or physicians. They also reject the "rational person" argument which defines the patient's desires by what a rational person under the same circumstances would decide.

Passive-Active Dimension

The second dimension of this euthanasia classification scheme describes the type of activity used to carry it out. Although, again, there certainly are many shades of distinction, most cases fall clearly into either passive or active categories. Passive euthanasia, currently the most prominent in public debate, is a decision to withhold or withdraw life-prolonging treatment from the patient. In this era of respirators and other artificial life-support technologies, the decision to forego life-sustaining treatment is becoming commonplace—although, since circumstances vary considerably, one must hope it will never become routine.

The Karen Quinlan case and others to be reviewed in this chapter have pushed passive euthanasia to the forefront of national interest in the last decade, spawning a multitude of state statutes designed to let individuals specify in advance their preference concerning acceptable and non-acceptable treatment if they ever reach the point where artificial life-support technologies are necessary. These natural-death laws have authorized "living wills" which contain legally recognized requests not to be kept alive on machines under specified conditions. As such, if carried out, they represent a form of voluntary passive euthanasia. Some opponents of voluntary passive euthanasia argue that allowing even hopeless patients the option of dying is the beginning of a "slippery slope" which will lead next to involuntary passive euthanasia and then to the killing of non-terminal patients like the mentally retarded or senile. In contrast, supporters argue that human beings have the right to die with dignity and to refuse treatment that would dehumanize them.

Passive euthanasia becomes harder to justify in speculative cases, in which the individual has given no express consent (either prior or immediate) to withhold lifesaving treatment. Baby Doe cases are prime examples of parents and physicians making life-death decisions in the absence of the defective infant's capacity to give consent. Similarly, when life-support systems are withheld from comatose patients, it is usually on the assumption that they would have chosen death over the alternative. Although the third parties in these cases might have the patient's interests at heart, they must rationalize their decision on the grounds that the patient, if able to decide, would have made the same choice. Such grounds are necessarily speculative, since one can never know for sure.

Involuntary passive euthanasia, the cessation of life-prolonging treatment to a conscious person against his or her will, is very difficult to justify morally or legally. In addition, it is contrary to the American medical tradition, which gives preference to patient autonomy. Despite these ethical difficulties, cost-benefit considerations may in the future place substantial pressure on the government to limit the amount of treatment that an individual can receive at public expense. Involuntary passive euthanasia raises the critical conceptual question of whether health and life are positive rights—that is, whether any individual can demand aggressive treatment and expect to receive it, whatever its cost to society. As the potential of life-prolonging technologies expands to artificial organs and an ever broader array of transplantation and regeneration techniques, this category of euthanasia is likely to become more commonplace.

Passive euthanasia, then, refrains from an action which could keep a person alive. In contrast, active euthanasia involves committing an act that leads directly to the death of the patient. In the medical setting this act is usually, though not always, a lethal injection. In several highly publicized cases, family members often frustrated by the medical profession's unwillingness to effectuate death through lethal injection, have shot their suffering spouse or parent. Recent television movies have sympathetically portrayed active euthanasia or mercy killing of persons with advanced stages of Alzheimer's disease.

As with the passive category, forms of active euthanasia can be distinguished according to the degree of consent by the patient. A woman with terminal cancer who convinces her husband to alleviate her pain by killing her, despite lingering questions of how free her decision really is under such traumatic circumstances, represents a case of active voluntary euthanasia. Opponents insist that this type of euthanasia is equivalent to suicide on the part of the patient and homicide by the person who carries it out. Contrarily, proponents argue that the right to die with dignity demands some degree of choice as to the circumstances of death, and they contend that the decision-making system has failed when it does not provide a painless and effective way of honoring a dying patient's wishes. But even if we could agree in principle that active voluntary euthanasia may sometimes be justified, consensus in many specific cases would be impossible (such as a patient who refuses to have a leg amputated and chooses to die instead, or a paraplegic or burn patient who demands the right to die).

Active speculative euthanasia, or the administration of death to a patient who is comatose or otherwise unable to give informed consent, raises the same questions as the passive speculative form, in addition to placing the participant in a position of actually performing the act that causes death. Active involuntary euthanasia raises even more questions of personal privacy and autonomy in life-death decisions. This form of euthanasia is currently unthinkable, partly because our legal system is designed primarily to protect against acts of commission, though not omission, and thus even those hospitals and other third parties that might consider passive involuntary euthanasia in the future are very unlikely to participate in a direct action, against the express wishes of the patient, resulting in that patient's death. Furthermore, active involuntary applications correctly reinforce allusions to Nazi Germany and raise legitimate concerns of a genocidal abuse of euthanasia. This category, and to a lesser extent the related active-speculative type, have no support in the United States. The evident inappropriateness of these two forms, however, should not color the genuine debate over the other four types.

Interestingly, the President's Commission on biomedical ethics consciously avoided the term "euthanasia" in its report *Deciding to Forego Life-Sustaining Treatment*. It argued (1983a:24) that terms such as *euthanasia* are "hopelessly blurred" and of little use in clarifying the issues. Presumably, the Commission also felt that the word would bring negative connotations to a procedure it was trying to place in a neutral context. "Foregoing life-sustaining treatment" simply sounds less threatening than "euthanasia" or "letting the patient die." Although the Commission's purposes, I believe, were well served by the exclusion of explicit uses of this word, I feel that the general term "euthanasia" has the heuristic advantage of providing a framework for comparing a broader set of conceptually connected applications. Politically, the Commission did what it had to do—for euthanasia still carries with it substantial emotional and controversial implications. Whatever term is used, the issues of euthanasia are becoming increasingly evident.

Euthanasia Policy

If we take the view that what is essentially human in the life that we share with the animal and vegetable kingdoms is the capacity for thought and love and aesthetic experience, and that this capacity makes us a person in the true sense of the word, we cannot wish to preserve an anonymous individual who has been stripped of personality and reduced by incessant pain or physical deterioration to the animal or vegetative level . . . yet without the medical assistance that voluntary euthanasia would authorize . . . it is unlikely that most of us would be able to choose a dignified death (Earl of Listowel, 1986).

The clamor for the right to die has become a matter of public policy, inextricably involving the legal system in decisions regarding several categories of euthanasia and taking shape as a political issue of increasing importance. Civil-liberties groups such as the American Civil Liberties Union (ACLU) have argued for individual autonomy in choosing to forego treatment. Interest groups such as the pro-euthanasia Hemlock Society and the Society for the Right to Die (SRD) lobby for legislation that would let an individual die with dignity. On the other hand, religious organizations, right-to-life groups, minority groups who see euthanasia as a threat to their interests, and some members of the medical profession oppose any action that legalizes the hastening of death.

Surveys of public opinion demonstrate an ambivalence toward euthanasia in general but considerable support for permitting individuals to discontinue the use of life-support technologies that prolong their life with no hope of recovery. A Gallup poll conducted for *Hospitals* magazine in December 1986 found that 70 percent of the respondents were "very willing" to have life-support systems discontinued and 12 percent were "somewhat willing," while only 18 percent were unwilling. Likewise, in a non-random poll by *Ladies Home Journal* in April 1987, 97 percent felt that terminally ill people have the "right to euthanasia." In the Gallup survey, 72 percent said they would be willing (46 percent "very willing") to disconnect artificial support systems on behalf of a relative. The proportion of the population opposed to passive voluntary euthanasia appears relatively small, though many of those opposed are very committed in their opposition.

The first major court case to engender public debate over the withholding of life-support systems was resolved in 1976. In *In re Quinlan,* the New Jersey Supreme Court ruled that Karen Quinlan, a young irreversibly comatose woman, had a right to die with dignity and permitted hospital authorities to remove her from the respirator. This decision ended over a year of efforts by Karen's parents to remove her from the life-support system and let her die in peace. The case was disputed in the media spotlight and served as a verbal battleground for groups on all sides of the issue. Importantly, the *Quinlan* ruling came just as many states were moving toward making brain function the criterion for determining when someone is legally dead. Because of the widespread publicity, *Quinlan* generated a multitude of legal actions to terminate extraordinary treatment.

In June 1987 the New Jersey Supreme Court expanded the guidelines it first handed down in *Quinlan*. In its rulings on three companion cases, the court supported a person's right to refuse to be kept alive by artificial means. Furthermore, the court extended the right to the friends and family of incompetent patients. The court stated, "The fateful decision to withdraw life-supporting treatment is extremely personal. Accordingly, a competent patient's right to make that decision will outweigh any countervailing state interests." Moreover, the incompetent patient who has previously expressed his or her wishes retains the right to refuse such treatment. The court granted civil and criminal immunity for close friends, relatives, or physicians who remove life-sustaining treatment from a patient who had asked not to be kept alive.

In the case of Nancy Ellen Jobes (age 31) the New Jersey court voted 6 to 1 that a relative or close friend may exercise the right of a patient in an "irreversibly vegetative state" to refuse life-sustaining medical treatment. Also by a 6-to-1 vote, the court ruled that the choice of an elderly nursing home patient (Hilda Peter, age 67) in a vegetative state who had left clear evidence of her desire to withhold extraordinary treatment must be respected, regardless of her life expectancy. By ruling that the likelihood of ever returning to "cognitive and sapient life," not life expectancy, is the important issue, the court expanded on its ruling in a 1985 case *(In re Conroy)* in which it had concluded that life-support apparatus may be removed from nursing-home patients who are in pain and who have a life expectancy of less than one year. The third case heard by the court in 1987 was that of Kathleen Farrell (age 37) who was declared competent (though she died before the court could rule in her case). In a 7-to-0 vote, the court said a competent person's interest in his or her self-determination generally outweighs any countervailing state interest.

Along similar lines, courts in an increasing number of states are ruling in favor of patients who desire to have their feeding tubes removed over the hospital's objections. The saga of Elizabeth Bouvia, a disabled patient whose request, in 1984, to be allowed to starve to death while in the hospital gained international attention, demonstrates the political sensitivity of these issues. (For a good summary of her case, see Humphry and Wickett, 1986.) This case also illustrates the difficulty of arriving at determinative decisions through the courts. Although the California Supreme Court unanimously rejected her original petition to be allowed to die, premising it on the fact that she was demanding in effect that the hospital directly contribute to her death by discontinuing what is "ordinary" treatment for persons in her condition, in 1986 after two years of legal maneuvering, Bouvia again sought a court order forbidding another hospital to force-feed her.

In a similar case in New York state, the state supreme court ruled that a man who was in extremely poor and deteriorating health, did *not* have to be force-fed. The court observed one key difference from Bouvia's case, though: G. Ross Henninger was 85 years old and had no chance to regain his health and return to his previous quality of life. In contrast, Elizabeth Bouvia although severely disabled, was 27 years old. This distinction leaves open the question of to what extent we should discriminate by age, health, or any other characteristic if the person requesting euthanasia is competent.

In June 1987, in a similar case *(Delio v. Westchester County Medical Center),* a New York appellate court found that the the patient alone has the right to reach the "ultimate decision" to refuse treatment and that there could be no countervailing interest in prolonging life by force-feeding which the patient would have found "demeaning and degrading to his humanity." What makes this case different is that Daniel Delio was in a permanent vegetative state, not legally competent to make the decision. The action to compel termination of tube feeding was brought by his wife, who argued that her husband (who had been a marathon runner) would not want to continue life in a condition that was the antithesis of all he believed in. Although the trial court questioned its authority to prohibit feeding a young (age 34) and what it termed "non-terminally ill patient," the appeals court ruled that the "panoply of rights associated with a competent person's right to self-determination" is not limited by reason of a person's age or medical condition. The court concluded: "We support the individual's right to refuse treatment and thereby live out his life in dignity and peace for whatever period of time remains."

Although there is still considerable variation among courts on this issue, the trend in case law clearly supports passive euthanasia in cases where the main decision is whether to initiate, continue, or terminate the use of artificial life-support systems. Much less clear is the issue of active euthanasia, as neither the courts nor the public have dealt extensively with mercy killing yet. Economic pressures promise to make active euthanasia a major issue in the coming decade.

Policy making on death-related issues stands approximately where abortion did in the early 1960s. The underlying need to reconsider society's traditional expectations as to suffering, terminal-illness procedures, and related matters brings euthanasia inexorably closer to the surface as a political issue. Sensationalized cases are essential to the process of politicalization, however. In the development of abortion politics, the growing subsurface dilemma of thousands of mothers faced with unwanted pregnancies required stimulation from the rubella and thalidomide tragedies (which led to thousands of malformed fetuses) to shake state legislatures into action. Karen Quinlan's and several other high-profile cases performed this function for euthanasia. Many states have passed natural-death laws since the 1970s, and constitutional considerations of equal protection will increasingly press the federal level of government toward nationwide standardization—much like that which *Roe v. Wade* provided for abortion.

As of 1987, 39 states had living-will laws. Of these, 18 had been enacted in the two previous years. Increasingly, these statutes are becoming standardized along the lines of the "Uniform Rights of the Terminally Ill Act" recommended by the National Conference of Commissioners on Uniform State Laws. Some states have replaced earlier living-will statutes with new, broadened laws. The Arkansas "Rights of the Terminally Ill or Permanently Unconscious Act," for instance, authorizes appointment of a health-care proxy to act on the patient's behalf when necessary and expands coverage to include permanently comatose patients as well as the terminally ill. (For an excellent summary of state living-will statutes see Society for the Right to Die [1987].)

In a related matter of policy, in light of the new capacities to sustain patients beyond the point where their life has any quality, the Joint Commission on Accreditation of Hospitals required all hospitals in the United States to establish, by January 1988, formal policies regarding resuscitation of terminally ill patients. Although many hospitals have had formal do-not-resuscitate (DNR) policies, many other facilities have instead depended on a confusing array of informal "no-code," "slow code," and "partial code" categories, generally with no provisions for patient consent. The failure by many hospitals to acknowledge their actions, often on grounds of potential liability, has acquired increasing policy importance because of the large number of potential candidates, now estimated at over 1.5 million per year.

The new standard requires consent from the patient and/or family before any decision to withhold cardiopulmonary resuscitation (CPR), which involves treatment of cardiac arrest by external chest compression and some form of artificial respiration. This requirement should reduce the procedural abuses that resulted from the absence of explicit DNR policy, and, by stipulating that written orders be documented in the patient's medical record, it should eliminate capricious, inconsistent approaches to these decisions. As Youngner (1987:24) has noted, however, this specific attention to DNR cases should not divert us from looking rigorously at other more common treatment-nontreatment decisions in the critical-care setting. Although CPR is a dramatic intervention, because it in effect brings the patient back to life after the traditional signs of death have appeared, we have seen that the range of life-sustaining technologies extends far beyond artificial resuscitation.

Alzheimer's Disease: A New Cause for Euthanasia?

The recent emphasis on the AIDS "epidemic" has overshadowed a disease category that will have increasing policy ramifications and create even greater economic costs: dementia, or senility. The most common form of dementia is Alzheimer's disease, which accounts for about two-thirds of all cases, although over 70 other disorders can cause dementia. In any form, dementia is a devastating illness and exacts a tremendous toll on the patient, family, and health-care system. Approximately three to six million Americans suffer from dementia, and the Office of Technology Assessment (1987b) estimates the cost of dementia to the nation in 1985 as between $24 and $28 billion—and growing rapidly.

Alzheimer's disease causes progressive deterioration of memory, intellect, language, emotional control, and perception. The disease is insidious, gradually progressing from subtle symptoms to almost complete mental deterioration. Victims in the advanced stages may be completely dependent on others for years or even decades, causing serious disruptions to the family and a huge financial burden. The number of persons affected by Alzheimer's disease is expected to double in the next decade, primarily because more and more people are living into their seventies or eighties, the age at which dementia usually strikes. The likelihood of developing dementia of some type is estimated at 20 to 30 percent for persons age 85 and over, as compared to only 1 percent for those between 65 and 74 and 7 percent for those age 75 to 84 (Cross and Gurland, 1987).

Although the cause of Alzheimer's disease is unknown, recent evidence suggests that at least some cases are inherited. Through the use of DNA probes to mark genes, researchers have linked the heritable form of Alzheimer's disease to chromosome 21, the same chromosome that causes Down's syndrome. As noted in chapter 3, the capacity to identify persons with a genetic predisposition toward Alzheimer's disease will eventually create new problems regarding use of that information. It is very unlikely, however, that we will have the capability to either prevent or cure this disease in the near future. According to Cook-Deegan and Whitehouse (1987:55), even if the most promising of drugs under consideration prove clinically useful, they will only delay onset of the disability or retard its progression.

Increasingly, patients with Alzheimer's disease and other forms of dementia will become candidates for euthanasia. Already spouses have killed their affected partner after watching him or her deteriorate to the point where they no longer could tolerate the transformation of their loved one to a vegetative state. Soon many living wills may include provisions stating that euthanasia, either passive or active, be carried out at a particular stage of mental deterioration. As with all forms of euthanasia, the gray areas between justifiable and unjustifiable cases are very large.

Redefining Death

Another issue with similar roots as euthanasia, although it has met less opposition, is the need to redefine death within the context of the new capacities to extend biological existence indefinitely. The President's Commission on bioethics concluded that "in light of ever increasing powers of biomedical science and practice, a statute is needed to provide a clear and socially-accepted basis for making definitions of death" (1981:i). While the Commission acknowledged the linkage of this issue to euthanasia, it concluded that, as matters of public policy, the two can be treated separately—thereby avoiding much of the emotional sensitivity that euthanasia arouses.

The traditional medical definition of death has been the permanent cessation of respiration and circulation. The situation used to be unambiguous, because once these functions ceased they could not be restored. But advances in medical techniques, which now permit machine-regulated breathing and heartbeat even when the capacity to breathe spontaneously is irreversibly lost, have made the traditional determination of death inadequate. Now the emphasis is on brain function as a criterion. Because the brain cannot regenerate neural cells, once the entire brain has been seriously damaged, spontaneous respiration can never return, even though breathing may be sustained by respirators or ventilators. The machines can maintain certain organic processes in the body, but they cannot restore consciousness.

This present situation, in which all bodily functions need not cease when the heart stops pumping, has led to the distinction between human life as a strictly biological existence and human life as an integrated set of social, intellectual, and communicative dimensions. Just what, we have had to ask, does it mean to be human? Perhaps surprisingly, a reasonably strong consensus has developed that recognizes the possibility of social or cognitive death even though the human organism is kept alive biologically by artificial means. However, some groups remain opposed to the movement toward recognizing brain death, and others who approve of the brain-death definition are uncomfortable with the dilemmas technology has created. Willard Gaylin's article on "Harvesting the Dead" (1974) opened a serious ethical debate on the status humanhood bestows even after death, however it is defined, occurs.

The first major step toward redefining death occurred in 1968, when rising concern by medical practitioners over how to treat respirator-supported patients led to creation of the "Harvard criteria" for brain death (Ad Hoc Committee, 1968). These criteria, developed by a Harvard Medical School committee, focused on (1) unreceptivity and unresponsiveness, (2) lack of spontaneous movements or breathing, and (3) lack of reflexes. Moreover, a flat electroencephalogram (EEG, a brain-wave test) showing no discernable electrical activity in the cerebral cortex was recommended as a confirmatory test, when available. All tests were to be repeated at least 24 hours later without demonstrable change before life-support systems could be terminated. These criteria, with some modifications and revisions due to new knowledge and diagnostic technologies, continue to serve as the medical criteria for determining brain death. Their publication led to the mobilizing of considerable support for legislating policy standards of brain death and eliminating the uncertainties faced by hospitals and physicians.

Another force at work during this period was the emergence of organ transplantation techniques and the growing need for organs. For transplants to be successful, a viable, intact organ is needed. The suitability of organs— especially the heart, lungs, and liver—for transplantation diminishes rapidly once the donor's respiration and circulation stop. Therefore, the most desirable donors are otherwise healthy persons who have died following traumatic head injuries and whose breathing and blood flow are artificially maintained until after the removal of the organs (President's Commission, 1981:23). Although advocates of the brain-death criterion downplay the extent to which the demand for organs influenced this movement, transplant-surgery did give the effort to define brain death a new urgency (Fox and Swazey, 1978). This reluctance to link the two developments is understandable, because the connection would imply that we have accepted the revised definition of death only to facilitate use of the "dead" individual's organs. Certainly, organ-transplant facilities have sought and have benefited from the legal clarity provided by statutes that define brain death. If the only rationale for this new definition of death was to facilitate successful organ transplants, however, support for brain death would be miniscule. As noted in chapter 4, recent efforts to maximize donation of usable organs notwithstanding, organs are procured for transplants in only a small percentage of the cases in which the brain-death criterion is applied.

Like most matters of public health, the determination of death traditionally has been within the province of each state's common law. This dependence on the courts to determine and apply the criterion for death has resulted in considerable uncertainty and a lack of consistency across jurisdictions. With patients often being transported across state lines for treatment, the lack of consistent policy produces confusion and potential for abuse. Two efforts to increase consistency have resulted: many state legislatures have enacted statutory standards, and a national standard has been proposed.

In 1970, the Kansas state legislature became the first to recognize brain-based criteria for determination of death. Within several years, four states passed laws patterned on the Kansas model. The Capron-Kass proposal (1972) offered the states a more succinct substitute that eliminated some of the Kansas model's ambiguity. To date, seven states have adopted the Capron-Kass model with minor modifications while three others have done so with more substantial changes. Two other model statutes (American Bar Association, 1975; National Conference of Commissioners on Uniform State Laws, 1978) have been enacted by five and two states, respectively. The American Medical Association's 1979 proposal, which includes extensive provisions to limit liability for persons taking actions under the proposal, has not been adopted in any state. About ten states have non-standard statutes that often include parts of one or more of these models, while about 20 states have no statutory determinations of death.

This proliferation of similar yet variant models and statutes led the President's Commission to propose a "Uniform Definition of Death Act." The Act provides for—

1. (Determination of Death.) An individual who has sustained either (1) irreversible cessation of circulatory and respiratory functions, or (2) irreversible cessation of all functions of the entire brain, including the brain stem, is dead. A determination of death must be made in accordance with accepted medical standards.

2. (Uniformity of Construction and Application.) This act shall be applied and construed to effectuate its general purpose to make uniform the law with respect to the subject of this Act among states enacting it (President's Commission, 1981:73).

Before its presentation in the final report, this uniform law was approved by the ABA, the AMA, and the Uniform Law Commissioners as a substitute for their original proposals.

The Commission recommended that uniform state statutes address general physiological standards rather than specific medical criteria or tests, since the latter continue to change with advances in biomedical knowledge and refined techniques. It concluded that "death is a unitary phenomenon which can be accurately demonstrated either on traditional grounds of irreversible cessation of heart and lung functions or on the basis of irreversible loss of all functions of the entire brain" (1981:1).

Although the Commission opted for total brain death (including the brain stem), not the cessation of selected functions, as its criterion, some argue that partial brain death is a better choice. Can a person be considered dead even though some parts of the brain remain alive? The brain stem can maintain the respiratory system even if the higher brain is not functioning, and the Commission contends that to declare dead a person who is spontaneously breathing yet has no higher brain functions would too radically change our definition of death. If, however, it is our higher brain functions that define us as humans, then partial brain death could be a more appropriate standard. As knowledge about the functioning of the brain increases, this issue may either dissipate or intensify. Currently whole brain death has consensual support among most experts and the public.

Whatever standards for determining death are used, they will remain troublesome for some persons. Despite the widespread policy of brain death across the states, thousands of legally brain-dead persons are kept alive by artificial means, usually at the request or demand of the family. The difficulty of letting go, the false hope for a miracle, and the confusion of values resulting from the new technologies cause many persons to refuse to authorize unplugging of the artificial life-support machines.

When such a situation exists, more tough questions arise. Can third-party payers, including Medicare and Medicaid, refuse to pay for care of a person who is legally dead? On what grounds can insurers justify such coverage? Can wills be probated in such a case? How can patients be protected from premature termination of helpful treatment under the guise of declaring death? What mechanisms are needed to maintain proper respect for the dignity of a brain-dead person when the various transplant teams need organs to save other patients who are brain-alive?

Although a few short years have powerfully transformed the meaning of death, many questions remain. Our very conception of what it means to be human are challenged by these rapid advances in medical technology. That these innovations present us with critical ethical policy decisions should not by itself be cause for alarm. It is when decisions of this magnitude become easy and coldly routine that we must all question our humanhood.

6 Policy Decisions in Biomedicine
Making Hard Choices

Biomedical technologies have forced our society to reexamine its most basic concepts of humanhood. These remarkable scientific advances, while they offer new hope for many persons and promise continued expansion of our capacity to control our own destiny and that of future generations, also challenge fundamental social values.

Our society has many hard biomedical policy choices to face, but perhaps the most basic and overarching questions concern the allocation of biomedical resources and the setting of health-care priorities, for the way we approach those issues will affect our use of all the specific technologies. This chapter examines these two key questions. It then turns to a short discussion of the policy issues raised by one illness that to date has no technological fix. Although in many ways AIDS is an atypical case of biomedical policy making, its high visibility makes it a useful case study illustrating the difficult choices we face in biomedicine.

Allocation of Biomedical Technology

As a society, the United States has been hesitant to institute policies limiting the amount of medical resources that can be committed to an individual. Cost-containment measures that attempt to set limits on individual care are widely attacked as contrary to the goals of health care. Meanwhile, the right to receive all available health care is reinforced by the press and successfully defended in the courts. This view that the individual's claim to medical resources ought to be predominant may keep us from making some hard health-care choices (Miller and Miller, 1986). Schramm (1984: 732) sees the status quo as leading to a "tyranny of our own making" through which we will "impoverish ourselves and successive generations by indulging in too much medicine." Market-driven solutions are bound to fail because they serve to reaffirm individual claims to resources and favor acute care for individuals, regardless of prognosis, over those measures which would improve the health status of the community as a whole. Schramm says the government can justifiably assert that the collective interest must take precedence over individual self-interest here. Within the liberal tradition, however, democratic institutions seem to face paralysis when abrogation of individual rights is imminent. It is clear that we must use our democratic institutions to stem the tide and regulate our overindulgence of medical care for the individual at all costs, but there is little evidence that the institutions are either willing or capable to execute such a change from above.

One reason why the government has responded so slowly to many of the policy problems discussed in this book centers on the major imbalance in the distribution of health-care benefits and costs across society. The benefits of the expanding health dollar are concentrated in a small but powerful segment of the economy—particularly for-profit health providers, which have flourished in recent years, in part because of the inflation of health costs—but its costs are diffused across many patients and third-party payers. As long as these costs were held within manageable bounds, the incentive for controlling inflation was much less than that for shifting costs to insurers. Congress's attempts to inhibit cost escalation have been aggressively opposed by a health-care industry that profits from the status quo.

Only recently have insurance companies exhibited concern over the long-term dangers of unbridled escalation of health-care costs, aggravated by the proliferation of expensive new technologies. Historically, insurers have, by and large, simply paid the costs and then passed them on to policy holders in the form of higher premiums. Because of tax incentives, themselves the products of successful lobbying by health-care providers and employers, health insurance continues to be heavily subsidized by the tax-payers. This policy has proved attractive to all parties, including most consumers, although it contributes to escalation of health costs and institutionalizes inequities between the middle-class professionals and union workers who enjoy comprehensive coverage as an untaxed fringe benefit and those groups without comparable coverage. Soaring insurance premiums, however, are causing a reevaluation on the part of all parties. Employers can no longer afford to provide comprehensive coverage to their employees. Employees are dissatisfied with the growing share of premiums they must pay and with the less complete coverage they enjoy. Finally, insurance companies are beginning to realize that costs can no longer simply be shifted to policy holders without grave long-term consequences.

One response to these unabated increases in cost would be to place strict limits on the use of these technological resources. Many forces, working concurrently, appear to be moving American society in the direction of government-supervised rationing of medical resources. David Mechanic (1977:3) cogently summarized the situation: "As people have learned to have high and more unrealistic expectations of medicine, demands for care for a variety of conditions, both major and minor, have accelerated. No nation that follows a sane public policy would facilitate the fulfillment of all perceptions of need that a demanding public might be willing to make. As in every other area of life, resources must be rationed."

The relevant question today is not whether we should ration health care but, rather, who ought to have prime responsibility for doing it. Physicians always have rationed medicine when resources available for treatment are scarce. Despite the predominance of the technological imperative (use all available technology) and ethical codes that emphasize benefit to the patient, doctors must allocate intensive-care resources, for instance, on the basis of the patient's prognosis (Detsky, Stricker, Mulley, and Thibault, 1981). Because the demand for ICU beds often outstrips availability, physicians must allocate them to patients who are most likely to benefit and deny such care to patients with the least favorable prognosis. In all medical decisions the criteria reflect social as well as medical factors. In addition to the treatment's likely outcome, itself always uncertain, the patient's preference and his or her potential future contributions to society are frequently considered. As a result, fewer resources are expended on the elderly and those persons with poorer prognosis, impaired functional status, or an unwillingness to fulfill expected social roles (Mulley, 1981:306).

Since any allocation decisions will make the difference between life and death for thousands of individuals, it is crucial that the criteria for making allocation decisions be clarified and carefully monitored to ensure that all members of society are served well by the health-care system. The need for sensitive handling of each individual is even more acute because many relationships in medicine, particularly those between patient and physician, have become more institutionalized, and because the high cost of many new medical technologies is likely to make their use prohibitive for many patients who might benefit or even for some who need the technology to live.

The enormity of the task of making contemporary biomedical policy means that government involvement will inevitably increase. Only the public sector has the capacity to reorder spending priorities and guide society toward moderating its unrealistic expectations. Unfortunately, too often in the past public institutions have played the opposite role and substantially raised expectations. Those persons who argue that competitive market forces, if left alone, will resolve these problems obscure the complexity of the issues and ignore the historical context of how we reached our present predicament. Joseph Califano (1986:82) undoubtedly is right that an "alert, informed world of business purchasers is one ingredient to the creation of an efficient health-care delivery system," but he dismisses too easily the essential role of the government in any such efforts. Although the private and public sectors must work together, I agree with Schramm (1984:731) that "only the government can act to redistribute opportunities for care in an equitable fashion and invest in public goods and services." The marketplace cannot possibly enable the just distribution of resources when the prime beneficiaries of the reordering of health-care priorities are members of future generations who have no means to influence today's marketplace. Initiative for change must come from those persons who supposedly represent the best interests of the nation as a whole.

The vigor with which public officials attack the health-care dilemmas and work to avert the emerging crisis will serve as a stern test of their commitment to justice. Allocation decisions concerning medical technologies are difficult and politically unpopular ones, but they will be made—either by government, by other leaders, or by default. Evans (1983:2208) is correct when he states; "Of all the resource-shortage crises this nation is expected to confront in the future, the problem of resource distribution is likely to be most acute and problematic in medicine."

Setting Limits on Health Care

As noted in chapter 1, our value system places heavy emphasis on the rights of citizens. Through a long series of rulings, the courts have consistently interpreted the right to life as including an inherent claim of citizens to health care and to a free choice in making health decisions. When rights and the common good conflict, the individual's claims to health care generally has taken precedence. Within the context of expanded technological possibilities and the accompanying costs, attention now has shifted to determining what, if any, limits should be placed on claims upon society by individuals for health care.

> As the cost of health care has escalated, our expectations of medicine have expanded. It seems that the more successful medicine becomes, the more we expect from it. In some quarters, the definition of health has expanded to include an all-inclusive concern for human well-being—physical, mental, and social. At the same time, the demands of "rights" to health and health care have extended to all segments of the population . . . . In addition to deciding how much of our resources will be committed to health care, we also must face the fact that full and complete care cannot be given to everyone in the society. By what system, then, shall individuals qualify? If exclusion is necessary, then by what system shall persons be excluded? (Harron, Burnside, and Beauchamp, 1983:114).

Many still believe that all persons in an affluent nation such as the United States should have a decent standard of health care and that society, has a duty to guarantee this standard to those who cannot afford it. But what does a "decent standard" of health care include and what might it exclude? The President's Commission on bioethics concluded that no one has the right to have life extended at all costs. Although everyone is "entitled to an adequate level of care," no one can demand a "maximum level that would bankrupt the nation," says Morris Abram, who chaired the Commission (President's Commission, 1983b:i). No one has the right to extraordinary health care if it requires public expenditures that preclude more basic health care for others. How to distinguish between ordinary and extraordinary care is, of course, a policy decision of great magnitude. As noted by Engelhardt (1984), there are moral as well as financial limits to society's ability to protect its members from the risks of poor health. The major policy problems center on what are the boundaries of health and who defines them.

Preventive Medicine and Lifestyle Change

Americans' preference for curative over preventive medicine has been well documented (Murray, 1984). This orientation is reinforced by the emphasis on the technological fix, the hesitancy to interfere with individual lifestyle choice, and the powerful momentum of the medical research community. Moreover, the medical profession has pursued the search for cures to disease more vigorously than ways to prevent disease. Often, however, the advanced technologies it develops are supportive rather than curative; that is, instead of curing a disease, they preserve a particular level of personal health by creating a continual dependence on further medical treatment (Ricardo-Campbell, 1982:6). Evidence suggests that the most significant improvements in health have come from preventive, not curative or supportive, medicine even though these latter efforts are the most dramatic and, therefore, most easily funded. Most advances in the preventive area, in turn, have come from areas outside medicine, primarily in improved sanitation, nutrition, housing, and education.

Although many proposed preventive efforts may not be cost-effective (Russell, 1986), when well planned and executed preventive medicine can provide a high return on its investment. Conversely, curative medicine is often of questionable utility, particularly near the end of the life cycle. Here again, though, society's obsession with prolonging life forces us to invest huge amounts of scarce health dollars in a quest to extend life even if only for a short time. Moreover, often the life we are saving is of low quality, spent attached to various tubes and machines in a sanitized hospital setting. The recent growth of hospice care and the frequent refusal of these heroic lifesaving measures represent a repudiation of the high-technology extensions of life that have become a major aspect of our "health" care system.

Despite this disenchantment with the prevailing focus on life extension at all costs, and the complaints that death has been dehumanized in the process, we continue to spend billions of dollars on the development of life-extending technologies. In the words of Lester Thurow (1985:611), "modern technology makes it likely that everyone will die of an illness that requires immense amounts of money except those lucky enough to die quietly in their sleep." The dominant ethos of the medical community as a whole, with strong support from the majority of the public, still favors curative medicine. Since health dollars expended in one area of medicine normally decrease availability of funds in other areas, this preoccupation with high-cost curative technologies raises serious questions about the allocation of funds. From a cost-effectiveness point of view, it is clear we are not making the best possible use of our limited health dollars. According to Saward and Sorensen (1980:49): "When viewed from an economic perspective, it would appear that in curative medicine we are spending more and more for less and less improvement." If, upon closer scrutiny, prevention proves more effective than curative efforts, then preventive medicine must become a high priority in a social policy that intends to distribute scarce resources most fairly. A multifaceted preventive approach necessitates that substantial attention be given to reducing environmental pollutants, eliminating unsafe working conditions, and improving housing, health-education, and early-detection programs. Inadequate nutrition also continues to contribute to a variety of health problems and must be addressed as part of a comprehensive health-care program.

The most difficult preventive measures are likely to be those in which the individual has prime responsibility: smoking, use of alcohol and drugs, diet, sedentary behavior, use of seat belts, and so forth. (For lack of a better term, these behaviors and habits are here labeled "lifestyle" decisions.) Attempts by the government to intervene in lifestyle decisions are inherently controversial. For instance, laws requiring motorcyclists to wear safety helmets have been attacked as paternalistic, unwarranted governmental interference in behavior that does not threaten the health of others. Many lifestyle mandates have been either rejected by the courts as violations of individual autonomy or rescinded by legislatures under constituency pressure. Nevertheless, pressures emerging from the coming health-care crisis demand that we consider much more closely (1) the role individuals play in contributing to their own health problems, (2) a shift of responsibility for health toward the individual, and (3) a renewed emphasis on individuals' obligations to society to do those things that maximize health.

To achieve these goals, we must begin by placing the social value of health at least on a par with that of enjoyment. The incentive structure operating within society must be radically revised to better reward healthful lifestyle choices by individual members. This effort must prominently entail reducing public expectations regarding the availability of health-care resources and, thereby, curtailing the unrealistic demand for curative medicine. Our consumptive society must realize the need for limits and dispense with its fatuous assumption of unlimited resources.

Any attempts to establish these attitudes and priorities through public policy will encounter stiff opposition. For instance, some persons suggest that the health-care crisis is largely an artifact of quantification techniques, such as cost-benefit analysis, that have become vehicles for "generating a crisis atmosphere in medicine" (Caplan, 1983:97). Others suggest that a different shift of societal priorities, such as a transfusion of dollars from the defense budget, would provide more than sufficient funds to resolve all our health-care funding problems. These critics contend that, to the extent that a health-care crisis exists, it is imposed by a government unwilling or unable to set the "proper" spending priorities. A reordering of these priorities, accompanied by the selection of health care for special emphasis, would provide adequate funds to handle the problems of health-care allocation. Finally, some observers (such as Ricardo-Campbell, 1982) explain that the major problem in health care today is overregulation. If the competitive market were left free to operate on its own, they argue, the dilemmas of medical care would dissipate.

Despite the apparent attractiveness of these arguments, they fail to reflect social or political reality. The health-care problem is a genuine one and is getting progressively worse. Whether or not one defines it as a crisis, medical care in the United States faces a bleak future unless substantial changes are forthcoming. Attributing these problems to inappropriate use of cost-benefit analysis or any other analytical approach misrepresents the clear trends in overall expenditures for health care as well as the means by which money is distributed. The scope of these problems is particularly large in organ transplantation and neonatal care.

Contentions that shifting funds from other areas of public spending to health care would solve the problem ignore two factors. First, whether or not one approves of U.S. military expenditures, there is little possibility that national defense funds soon will be transferred to social programs. Even if there were, health would have to compete with other potential recipient areas. Under the current deficit budgetary conditions, cuts, not increases, in health care spending as a proportion of the federal budget are likely. Second, even if the improbable happened and the government decided to trade defense priorities for health care, history indicates that the appropriation of additional funds to medicine often exacerbates rather than resolves the problems. Because health-care needs and demands are virtually unlimited and funding sources are finite, shifting higher proportions of the gross national product or the federal budget to medicine serves simply to postpone that inevitable point at which constraints must be imposed. Although the government has the means to initiate and coordinate necessary action, it cannot succeed without explicit support from health-care providers and the consumer public.

Unfortunately, neither patients nor physicians are doing much about increased costs, improving the rationale behind allocation of health-care services, or even asking the difficult questions about the value of existing patterns in medicine (Mechanic, 1981:83). The current structure of third-party reimbursement favors the allocation of more health-care resources than would be needed if patients bore a larger proportion of the costs for the benefits they accrued (Newhouse, Manning, Morris, Orr, and Dean, 1981). Consumers of health care currently assess their medical needs without considering the full price, and because needs largely define demand, this situation creates an inherent bias in the system toward increased allocation of resources. Although a large proportion of the public agrees that cost containment in health care is essential, these people are not as willing to sacrifice benefits they presently hold in order to reduce the overall costs to society, and very few are willing to make drastic lifestyle changes out of a responsibility to reduce the overall cost of health care in the United States. They seem to expect the cost to be reduced at the expense of others or assume that the government can bear these costs.

The Role of the Biomedical Community in Biomedical Policy

Even more critical than the general public's support for resource allocation is the cooperation of the health care-profession, which itself is highly factionalized. No health program can succeed without at least tacit support from physicians, hospitals, and other health-care providers. Physicians are particularly key decision makers on the demand side of medicine, since they serve as gatekeepers for access to treatment regimens, technologies, and drugs. "Physicians are logical agents of rationing because they appear to have direct control over health care dollars" (Dyer, 1986:5). Mulley (1981:300) argues that physicians' relatively subjective decisions about patients' needs largely determine the demand for expensive intensive-care treatment and tend to become institutionalized in the administrative decisions of hospitals and planning agencies. Staff doctors, for instance, encourage the use of intensive-care units (ICUs) because they want maximum health care to be readily available for their patients should the need arise—not because they want to maintain a minimal occupancy rate in ICU beds. But as more ICU beds become available, patients with less severe diseases are likely to be admitted, despite questions about these units' effectiveness (Hill, Hampton, and Mitchell, 1978:289). Also, the combined impact of fee-for-service payments and third-party reimbursement gives hospitals a natural incentive to respond aggressively to their patients' perceived needs.

Any government attempt to require physicians to allocate medical care on grounds of society's rather than simply the patient's need is bound to conflict with professional ethics and the traditional patient-physician relationship. Pellegrino (1986) argues that any steps taken to make the physician the designated guardian of society's resources are morally unsound and factually suspect. According to Aaron and Schwartz (1984), this approach would require a far-reaching attitude change for those many physicians who believe it is unprofessional, if not immoral, to consider costs in deciding what actions to take on behalf of patients. Loewy (1980:697) concludes that economic considerations as they affect either the patient, the hospital, or society are "not germane to ethical medical practice" and that it is "dangerous" to introduce such extraneous factors into medical decisions. Dyer (1986:6) answers "an emphatic 'No'" in answer to the question of whether the physician can be society's agent in reducing health costs. Allocation decisions should not be made by doctors at the bedside, he says, because their primary responsibility is to the patient, not society: "To ask conscientious physicians to bear the responsibility for lowering the cost of medical care is to create a conflict of interest that threatens to alter the nature of the doctor-patient relationship and the nature of the medical profession itself " (Dyer, 1986:6). For these reasons, the medical profession in the United States is unlikely to develop norms that require or actively encourage rationing (Schuck, 1981).

Despite its hesitency, however, the medical profession increasingly will find itself in the difficult position of responding to government initiatives and, eventually, to public pressures to make difficult allocation and rationing decisions. Physicians have always made such decisions (e.g., who gets an ICU bed if the ICU is full) on a case-by-case basis, at the bedside, or in the hospital administrator's office—not under governmental pressure or in a systematic, institutionalized manner. Their central commitment has been to the patient, not society, and the current shift toward public allocation poses a clear threat to traditional medical ethics. Harrison Rogers, in his address as outgoing president of the American Medical Association, warned against this threat as reflected in a "very serious movement" toward maintaining a business ethic in medical practice rather than a professional ethic devoted primarily to protecting patients.

> Almost every force being exerted on doctors today is pushing them away from the professional aspects of what they do, and toward the business aspects. Governmental DRG [Diagnosis-related group] programs, reductions made in Medicare benefits and payments, restrictions on private plans, preadmission certification, second opinion requirements, requirements for outpatient, and ambulatory care—all of those and many others tend to make the doctor think first about the financial aspects of the needed services, and whether the patient or a governmental or private third party will be willing or able to pay for them (Rogers, 1986:4).

Lundberg (1983:2224) rhetorically asks how long physicians can continue to make such difficult policy judgments in response to short-term pressures of the moment. Can this piecemeal rationing process continue to dominate in light of the extensive social investment riding on each decision?

In contrast, Hiatt (1975) argues that the medical profession must take responsibility for evaluating expensive new medical technologies and techniques before they are made available to consumers. Because of their crucial role as the point of access to health care, Hiatt asserts, doctors must regulate the supply of medical services as a means of cost control. No longer do health-care providers automatically have a claim to all the societal resources they believe might benefit their patients, nor should they be able to make allocation decisions without an awareness of the complex ramifications of those decisions for the health-care system as a whole. As uncomfortable as this change may be to the medical profession, it is well underway in American society. Moreover, this shift is beginning to occur despite the lack of significant government involvement in the allocation of medical care. It is most directly evident in trends toward corporate health care, health maintenance organizations, and the increased allocation role played by benefits managers for large U.S. employers.

The most scarce resource in the health-care system in the future may not be money or expensive equipment, but specialized personnel. Recently, the acute shortage of intensive-care nurses has caused sudden decreases in the availability of intensive-care beds and some types of surgery. Pinkney (1987:1) cites a federal government prediction of a shortage of 1.2 million registered nurses by the year 2000 as but one example of shortages in many areas of hospital employment, from physical therapists to laboratory technicians. Highly trained personnel for transplant operations, although sufficient in most locales under present surgical loads, will be in short supply if transplantation facilities continue to multiply, as is inevitable under current public policy.

Although the shortage of nurses and other highly specialized support personnel is in part a function of limited budgets reflected in low salaries, it also has roots in the conflict between the traditional role of nursing as primary care and the accelerating movement toward specialized, machine-dependent medicine. Within this allocation context, it often is less difficult to secure initial funding for the purchase of prohibitively expensive medical technologies than to pay for the continuing personnel costs required to use and maintain the equipment. This short-sighted approach to expenditure decisions results in situations where a facility cannot use its most advanced equipment because of staffing shortages. This underuse of existing technology is especially frustrating because it represents a waste of substantial investments that could have been put to more productive use. As long as new-equipment expenditures take priority over the more mundane and routine operation of medical facilities, shortages of highly trained and motivated support personnel will intensify. Substantially more attention must be directed toward this problem in allocating medical resources.

The AIDS Problem: *A Case Study*

No problem in American health care today illustrates the inseparable tie between medicine and politics more vividly than AIDS. In addition to the arduous allocation decisions that will seriously aggravate the already precarious economic context of health care, AIDS raises critical ethical, political, and constitutional questions. The prevalence of homosexuals and intravenous drug users among AIDS victims heightens the controversy surrounding any policies designed to control the spread of this disease. The fact that the primary mode of transmittal is sexual intercourse further introduces a moral dimension not present in many other diseases. Finally, because this disease is always fatal, the stakes are considerably higher than for most other communicative diseases. The importance and sensitivity of AIDS, requires a specific discussion of the unique policy questions raised by this disease.

The AIDS virus, now known by convention as the human immunodeficiency virus (HIV), is transmitted through bodily fluids such as semen and blood. It enters the blood through sexual intercourse, transfusions, or contaminated needles. Although other routes of infection (such as exchange of saliva) are theoretically possible, there no data suggesting that HIV is transmitted via casual contact with an infected person. As we will see, this is a critical factor in framing AIDS policy.

One area of confusion with critical policy ramifications is the distinction between carrying the virus and having AIDS. A person may test positive for HIV antibodies upon being exposed to the virus but still exhibit no symptoms of the disease. It is estimated that there might be as many as 2 million carriers of AIDS (i.e., people who have the virus) in the U.S., but of these only a small percentage have the disease itself. A larger proportion have developed AIDS-related complex (ARC), a less lethal illness caused by the virus.

There continues to be disagreement over what proportion of those persons who test positive for HIV antibodies will contract ARC or AIDS. Part of this controversy stems from the uncertainty of the incubation period for

AIDS—that is, how long it takes the virus to give rise to the disease. We do know that most of the adults who have died of AIDS as of 1988 were infected early in the decade, but we do not know how many more who were infected then will die in the future.

Early studies estimated that only 5 to 10 percent of persons with HIV would develop AIDS. However, further data have caused this estimate to be revised upward. The Institute of Medicine (1987:93) suggests that at least 25 to 50 percent of infected persons will progress to AIDS within 5 to 10 years of infection, and "The possibility that the percentage may be higher cannot be ruled out." Based on extrapolations from current data, Harris (1987:61) estimates that 40 percent of infected persons will contract AIDS within seven years and 53 percent within fifteen years, even though only 4 percent have developed AIDS within three years. He also suggests that the different affected groups studied (homosexuals, hemophiliacs, transfusion patients) may have a different rate and incubation periods.

The skyrocketing costs of AIDS have become a major issue (Fox, 1987). In a study conducted in 1985 by the Centers for Disease Control (Hardy, Rauch, Echenberg, Morgan, and Curran, 1986), the lifetime hospital costs of the first 10,000 AIDS patients were estimated as totaling $1.473 billion, or $147,000 per patient, and the indirect costs attributable to loss of productivity were set at $4.8 billion. Because AIDS patients are predominantly young males, the indirect cost in lost production and future earnings is unusually high. Scitovsky and Rice (1987) estimate that by 1991, the annual cost of personal medical care for AIDS patients in the United States will have reached $8.5 billion, with another $2.3 billion being spent on non-personal costs such as screening, education, and research. They also predict that the indirect costs of AIDS will jump well over tenfold by 1991, to $55.6 billion.

Actually, due to the comparatively small number of patients so far, the cost of AIDS is still much lower than that of other, more common illnesses such as cancer and heart disease. In 1985, the personal medical costs of AIDS represented only 0.2 percent of the total personal health-care expenditures in the United States. Based on the estimate of Scitovsky and Rice (1987:5), even by 1991 this percentage will only increase to 1.4 percent. However, the severe strain AIDS cases have already placed on health-care resources in a few urban areas, especially New York and San Francisco, suggests that the tremendous increase in AIDS cases projected over the next five years will make this disease a critical economic burden to the nation. The total number of AIDS patients alive at any time during the year rose from 9,368 in 1984 to 18,720 in 1985 and 31,440 in 1986. It is expected to reach 172,800 by 1991.

As we have seen, the AIDS crisis comes at a time when monies are scarce even for established health programs. AIDS will further aggravate the economic choices and heighten the political factors involved as affected groups demand more governmental support and services. Because of the high cost per patient, the financial burden on the victims of AIDS and their families is crushing. Those affected will clamor loudly and emotionally for economic and political assistance.

One of the earliest steps in the quest to fight AIDS after it emerged in 1981 was the development of a test to identify persons who had been exposed to the virus. Since all persons infected with HIV develop antibodies to it, this enzyme-linked immunosorbant assay (ELISA), which detects antibodies to HIV, provided the means to test individuals and screen populations. ELISA is a relatively easy and inexpensive test. Although it does not identify HIV directly, it can identify who has been exposed to it.

As we saw in our discussion of genetic testing (chapter 2), however, the presence of an accurate, inexpensive test creates policy issues concerning its proper use (Blaine, 1987:2). Because AIDS is concentrated in identifiable high-risk groups, any screening efforts targeted at those groups threaten to cause stigmatization. If insurance companies and employers have access to such information, discrimination is likely (Scherzer, 1987). Because there is no AIDS vaccine and no way to protect the health of those who test positive, justification of mandatory screening has to be based on the premise that such testing will lead to modification of their behavior. Opponents of mandatory screening for AIDS, however, point out that it is unlikely to lead to the behavior changes needed to impede the spread of AIDS (Gostin and Curran, 1987:361). Under such circumstances, it is difficult to justify invading the privacy of so many persons.

Proponents of mandatory screening for HIV reply, however, that public health takes precedence over individual privacy, particularly when the disease is fatal. This argument has convinced the U.S. military, the Department of State, and the Department of Labor to initiate mandatory screening programs (Hummel, 1987). Furthermore, several states have passed, and others are considering, laws that would require premarital testing for

AIDS; screening in prisons, hospitals, or drug dependence clinics; and sur-
veillance and contact testing. Often these proposals have been advocated
(and passed) despite opposition from health professionals.

The economic pressure on insurance companies and employers to identify and exclude people at risk for AIDS is growing, and the debate as to
whether these organizations should be permitted to use HIV testing for
routine screening of applicants is intense. Harris (1987) argues that if employers, insurance companies, and prospective sex partners are not allowed to use the blood test, they may resort to such crude substitutes as
marital status, location of residence, history of hepatitis, and low white
blood cell counts as ways of identifying those infected. This will deny
many unaffected as well as infected persons access to jobs and insurance
coverage. "In the end, it will be a choice: use the HIV-antibody test or let
these cruder tests prevail" (Harris, 1987:64). Either way, those who test
positive will become an underclass, according to Harris.

Discrimination against persons who test positive for HIV is already very
real. The general public has not clearly understood the distinction between
testing positive for HIV and having AIDS. Affected children have had to
obtain court orders to attend school, and in at least one case physical in-
timidation was used against their parents. This near-hysteria about AIDS
among some segments of the population is not surprising in light of the
rapid and sensational way in which AIDS became a top media story. The
experts' early ambivalence concerning modes of transmission, incubation
period, and most recently the effectiveness of preventive measures does
not instill confidence in a public who has been told that AIDS represents an
epidemic rivaling the Black Plague. As Singer and Rogers (1986:12) put it:
"Finally, vagueness and contradiction in the advice offered by scientists
and public health officials contribute to a climate in which fear
flourishes. . . . And because AIDS is a new disease with many unknowns,
the advice that is given has changed over time, and at times different authorities offer differing advice. This too contributes to a climate of fear."
The emphasis in the mid-1980s on AIDS's spread to the heterosexual community did much to fuel public concern, despite public-health officials' in-
sistence that AIDS could not be spread by casual contact.

Because prevention of AIDS and rational, humane treatment of its vic-
time (and HIV carriers) depend so heavily on public cooperation, the way
in which the public perceives the threat will have a considerable impact on

how health officials respond to AIDS. In 1987 the Surgeon General and public-health officials initiated a major effort to educate the public on the facts of AIDS and on prevention. The widespread anxiety fueled by continual uncertainty, skepticism, and fear of this deadly disease will not easily abate, however. As a result, any AIDs proposals or policies will elicit public controversy. "Issues presented by the AIDS crisis are not new to medical ethics. Issues such as distributive justice, privacy, duties to third parties, experimentation, or respect for human dignity have been at the center of bioethical and public policy debates. The AIDS crisis has only made them more urgent" (Quist, 1987:2).

If AIDS were striking the general population indiscriminately, the main policy problems would center on allocation of resources. If AIDS were communicated primarily by casual contact, its victims would receive substantial public sympathy. In contrast, the concentration of AIDS among two groups who enjoy little public support—homosexuals and heroin addicts—intensifies the constitutional issues surrounding efforts to control AIDS. With the homosexual lifestyle already facing condemnation from many in society, and with heroin addicts enjoying little sympathy from either the public or health professionals, blaming the AIDS victim for his own problem has been popular. Not surprisingly, the distinction between the "innocent" victims of AIDS (such as blood transfusion recipients or children) and those whose lifestyles led to their infections became engrained in the public dialogue over AIDS. The attempts by the Centers for Disease Control (CDC) and the Surgeon General to shift emphasis to the threat of AIDS to the heterosexual community despite a lack of clear evidence may represent an effort to defuse the blame-the-victim approach.

Additionally, as new cases of AIDS among intravenous (IV) drug users have begun to outnumber those among homosexuals, another politically explosive pattern of infection is apparent. Although blacks make up 12 percent and Hispanics 6 percent of the U.S. population, they represent, respectively, 25 percent and 12 percent of persons with AIDS. From an economic standpoint, these people are least likely to be able to afford the cost of the disease. From a social standpoint, these minorities, who already suffer from discrimination, are highly vulnerable to further stigmatization and invasion of privacy in the name of public health. Any attempts to screen for AIDS that target these high-risk groups will face constitutional challenges on the basis of due process and equal protection of the law.

In March 1987, the U.S. Supreme Court ruled 7 to 2 that antidiscrimination laws do apply to individuals with contagious diseases *(School Board of Nassau Co. Fla. v. Arline)*. Although this case dealt specifically with the dismissal of an employee who had tuberculosis, the ruling that communicable diseases are disabilities included under Section 504 of the Rehabilitation Act of 1973 is also applicable to AIDS patients. Employers cannot fire or otherwise discriminate without putting the burden of legal proof on themselves. Furthermore, if they fail to keep HIV test results confidential, they may be held liable for libel or slander.

Under this court ruling, any exclusion of persons with a contagious disease from the protection of the Rehabilitation Act, must be based on sound medical evidence of risk to others, not on irrational fears. In the words of Justice William J. Brennan, Jr., writing for the majority, the law's basic purpose is to "ensure that handicapped individuals are not denied jobs or other benefits because of the prejudiced attitudes or the ignorance of others." Although significant legal action over aspects of these questions will continue, the explicit recognition of AIDS as a handicap under federal law assures some degree of legal protection of persons who test positive for HIV or have AIDS. In no way, however, does it eliminate discrimination against AIDS patients in housing, insurance, or personal relationships, nor does it specify how concerns for danger to the public health should be balanced with individuals' right to privacy. In short, the battle between individual rights and societal good within the context of AIDS is far from over. Related issues of exclusion of children from public schools, the testing and quarantining of prostitutes, and transmission of AIDS to children in utero will provide an expanding array of court cases in the coming decade.

AIDS stymies our technologically oriented society because there is no technological fix for it. Most experts express guarded hope at best for medical breakthroughs in stemming the spread of AIDS within the next decade (Institute of Medicine, 1987:99). This means that, at least for the near future, the only effective measure for reducing the spread of HIV infection is to educate the public, particularly those individuals at higher risk.

The realization that we cannot count upon a technical breakthrough has finally caused us to focus on prevention. Placing the policy emphasis on prevention, however, naturally centers the spotlight on identifiable groups whose members are at high risk—segments of the population who, as noted above, are already the subject of stigmatization. Furthermore, because of the nature of AIDS transmission, prevention efforts must demand drastic changes in these individual's behavior, thereby escalating invasion-of-privacy problems and the political difficulties of implementing the policy. Finally, stressing prevention too heavily could leave AIDS policy open to the charge of failing to respond adequately to the needs of those who have already contracted the disease.

We urgently need a national AIDS policy that encompasses significant funding for education, research, and health services. To date, as with the biomedical applications discussed in earlier chapters, there has developed instead a confusing array of state statutes and administrative regulations, with conflicting policies often apparent even within single jurisdictions. While some states have initiated rigid screening programs of varying categories of persons, from prisoners to marriage license applicants, other states have passed no legislation. In 1987 alone, over 450 bills on AIDS were introduced in state legislatures (Lewis, 1987:2410). Of the laws that passed, seven have premarital screening provisions, five mandate testing of prisoners, and twenty specify reporting procedures for HIV. This inconsistent policy framework results in considerable inequity in government efforts to deal with AIDS. To some extent, this fragmented policy is the result of the geographical imbalance of AIDS cases thus far. However, as the acute severity of the problem expands beyond New York, San Francisco, and Los Angeles and extends across the country, consistent policy will be essential. The debates over insurance and HIV testing are but two of the issues that demand a credible, national AIDS policy forum (Hummel, 1987).

Although the sensational aspects of AIDS attracted an inordinate amount of early attention to this disease, its continuing spread will make AIDS a central political issue of the 1990s, thus dramatizing the public-policy dimensions of all the biomedical issues we have discussed. Unfortunately, even our limited advances in our medical knowledge of AIDS have outdistanced our capacity to deal with its sociopolitical aspects. AIDS is at least as much a policy challenge as a technological one. The media's gripping, still proliferating AIDS reports, like the stories of transplants, test-tube babies, and genetic intervention, remind us regularly that biomedicine promises to present American society with some of the most difficult policy choices imaginable. How well we handle them will depend largely on how successful we are in informing and educating our citizens on these critical issues.

Firm Foundations: *The Central Questions of Biomedical Policy*

As a result of our society's deeply rooted dependence on biomedical technology to cure our ills, biomedicine will continue to progress faster than policy can catch up to it. The most rapid advances are likely to occur in the areas of genetic intervention, organ transplantation, neonatal intensive care, and brain intervention. Extensions of current technologies—including brain cell transplants from fetuses, organ transplants from anencephalic newborns, and interspecies organ transplants—are bound to raise increasingly complex ethical dilemmas and intensify the policy dimensions of biomedical technology.

As technology progresses, though, four basic types of policy questions will remain crucial. First, what level of technological intervention is appropriate for a given problem? How far should we seek to go in controlling our own destiny, in our quest for technological fixes to extend life? Gene therapy to enhance human capabilities and expanded forms of life-prolonging technological intervention will keep this question in prominence. So will the increasing numbers of people who are unwilling to let technology dictate how they die and are taking action through living wills to limit such intervention at that stage.

Second, who should determine whether a particular technology should be developed, should be funded, or should be applied in a specific case? Pressures for governmental controls, even though they threaten the traditional physician-patient relationship and personal autonomy, will increase due to tightening economic constraints. In this era of scarce resources, in part brought on by the high-cost technologies themselves, we can no longer assume that just because a technology is available we can or should use it. I feel strongly that the government must be intimately involved in setting priorities for use of these technologies.

The role of the government becomes even more crucial regarding the question of how to allocate and distribute biomedicine. Should these technologies be equally available to all persons? The traditional market-oriented, third-party payer system leaves many people out. The debate over whether or not the government has a responsibility to pay for expensive treatments when the individual cannot will intensify even more as the potential interventions increase. The ongoing policy battle over who should pay for liver transplants and the emerging demands for government funding of reproductive technologies illustrate the perplexing nature of this dilemma within our political value system. Can we ever justifiably choose not to save the life of an individual who needs a liver transplant when the technology and the new organ are available? What if that person's abuse of alcohol directly caused the condition? What criteria do we use to determine who gets scarce resources? The direct life-or-death implications of these choices for many individuals makes them qualitatively different from typical allocation and rationing decisions.

The fourth central policy question we must address is the impact on society of the use of each new technology. Once a technology becomes widely used, it is usually too late to place limits on its use. Technology assessment must anticipate negative long-term social consequences of any medical intervention before tempting society with that intervention's short-term benefits. Although the government's assessment efforts have increased substantially in the last decade (see chapter 1), they are constrained by a value system that largely favors technological progress. As a result, the difficult choices of rejecting specific technologies because of their negative social consequences are not made.

Our society must begin to set its priorities more objectively and recognize that we cannot afford to proceed full speed ahead on the development and use of all biomedical technologies. We must realize that the rapid advances in biomedicine, and the many real benefits that accompany them, are inseparable from equally real problems and costs. We can no longer afford to blindly embrace technology for its own sake. Instead we must carefully assess the long-term implications of each application before we use it.

Bibliography

Aaron, Henry J., and William B. Schwartz (1984). *The Painful Prescription: Rationing Hospital Care.* Washington, D.C.: The Brookings Institute.

Adams, Mellisa M., Godfrey P. Oakley, and James M. Marks (1982). "Maternal Age and Births in the 1980s." *Journal of the American Medical Association* 247:493–498.

Ad Hoc Committee of the Harvard Medical School to Examine the Definition of Brain Death (1968). "A Definition of Irreversible Coma." *Journal of the American Medical Association* 205:337.

American Academy of Pediatrics (1984). "Guidelines Announced for Infant Bioethics Committees." *News and Comment* 35(6):1.

American Bar Association (1975). *A.B.A. Annual Report* 100:221–232.

Anderson, W. French (1984). "Prospects for Human Gene Therapy." *Science* 226:401–409.

Andrews, Lori B. (1984). *New Conceptions: A Consumer's Guide to the Newest Infertility Treatments.* New York: St. Martin's.

Annas, George J. (1981). "Righting the Wrong of 'Wrongful Life.'" *Hastings Center Report* 11:8.

———— (1982). "Forced Cesareans: The Most Unkindest Cut of All." *Hastings Center Report* 12(3):16–17, 45.

———— (1985). "The Prostitute, the Playboy, and the Poet: Rationing Schemes for Organ Transplantation." *American Journal of Public Health* 75(2):187–189.

Ashford, Nicholas A., and Charles C. Caldart (1983). "The Control of Reproductive Hazards in the Workplace: A Prescription for Prevention." *Industrial Relations Law Journal* 5:523–563.

Austen, W. Gerald, and A. Benedict Cosimi (1984). "Editorial Retrospective: Heart Transplantation After Sixteen Years." *New England Journal of Medicine* 311(22):1436–1438.

Bayer, Ronald (1982). "Women, Work, and Reproductive Hazards." *Hastings Center Report* 2(5):14–19.

Beckwith, Jon (1976). "Social and Political Uses of Genetics in the United States: Past and Present." *Annals of the New York Academy of Sciences* 265:46–58.

Benacerraf, Beryl R., Rebecca Gelman, and Fredric D. Frigoletto (1987). "Sonographic Identification of Second-Trimester Fetuses with Down's Syndrome." *Journal of the American Medical Association* 317(22):1371–1376.

Biggers, John D. (1978). "In Vitro Fertilization, Embryo Culture and Embryo Transfer in the Human," Unpublished paper prepared for the Ethics Advisory Board, Department of Health, Education, and Welfare, Washington, D.C.: Government Printing Office, Appendix 8.

Bingham, Eula (1980) "Some Scientific and Social Hazards of Identifying Reproductive Hazards in the Workplace." In Peter F. Infante and Marvin S. Legator, eds., *Proceedings of a Workshop on Methodology for Assessing Reproductive Hazards in the Workplace*. Washington, D.C.: National Institute for Occupational Safety and Health. Pp. 3–6.

Bishop, Jerry E., and Michael Waldholz (1986). "The Search for a Perfect Child." *Wall Street Journal,* (March 19): 1.

Blaine, Jack H. (1987). "AIDS: Regulatory Issues for Life and Health Insurers." *AIDS and Public Policy Journal* 2(1):2–9.

Blank, Robert H. (1981). *The Political Implications of Human Genetic Technology.* Boulder: Westview Press.

——— (1986). "Emerging Notions of Women's Rights and Responsibilities during Gestation." *Journal of Legal Medicine* 7(4):441–469.

——— (1988). *Rationing Medicine.* New York: Columbia University Press.

Blendon, Robert J. (1986). "Health Policy Choices for the 1990s." *Issues in Science and Technology* 2(4):65–73.

Bolognese, R. (1982). "Medico-Legal Aspects of a Human Life Amendment." *Pennsylvania Law Journal Reporter* 5:13.

Bosy, Linda (1987). "A Cold 'Nuclear Winter': Blood Bankers Collect Fewer Units as Tests, Lack of Donors Threaten Volunteer System." *American Medical News* (February 20):2,17.

Bowes, Watson A., and Michael Simmons (1980). "Improved Outcome in Very Low-Birth Weight Infants." *American Journal of Obstetrics and Gynecology* 136(8):1080.

Brandon, William P. (1982). "Health-Related Tax Subsidies: Government Hand-outs for the Affluent." *New England Journal of Medicine* 307(15):947–950.

Brock, D. J. H., A. E. Bolton, and J. M. Monaghan (1973). "Prenatal Diagnosis of Anencephaly through Maternal Serum Alpha-Fetoprotein Measurement." *The Lancet* 1973(2):923–924.

Budiansky, Stephen (1987). "Playing Roulette With Experimental Drugs." *U.S. News and World Report* (July 13):58–59.

Califano, Joseph A., Jr. (1986). "A Corporate Rx for America: Managing Runaway Health Costs." *Issues in Science and Technology* 2(3):81–90.

Caplan, Arthur L. (1983). "How Should Values Count in the Allocation of New Technologies in Health Care?" In Ronald Bayer, Arthur L. Caplan, and Norman Daniels, eds., *In Search of Equity: Health Needs and the Health Care System*. New York: Plenum Press.

Capron, Alexander M. (1975). "Legal Issues in Fetal Diagnosis and Abortion." In Charles Birch and Paul Abrecht, eds., *Genetics and the Quality of Life*. Australia: Pergamon Press. Pp. 120–129.

——— (1979). "Tort Liability in Genetic Counseling." *Columbia Law Review* 79:619–684.

Capron, Alexander M., and Leon R. Kass (1972). "A Statutory Definition of the Standards for Determining Human Death: An Appraisal and a Proposal." *University of Pennsylvania Law Review* 121:87–104.

Chorover, Stephen L. (1981). "Psychosurgery: A Neuropsychological Perspective." In Thomas A. Mappes and Jane S. Zembaty, eds., *Biomedical Ethics*. New York: McGraw-Hill. Pp. 286–293.

Coates, J. F. (1978). "What is a Public Policy Issue?" In Kenneth R. Hammond, ed., *Judgment and Decision in Public Policy Formation*. Boulder: Westview Press.

Cohen, Ellis N. (1980). "Waste Anesthetic Gases and Reproductive Health in Operating Room Personnel." In Peter F. Infante and Marvin S. Legator, eds., *Proceedings of a Workshop on Methodology for Assessing Reproductive Hazards in the Workplace*. Washington, D.C.: National Institute for Occupational Safety and Health. Pp. 69–86.

Cook-Deegan, Robert M., and Peter J. Whitehouse (1987). "Alzheimer's Disease and Dementia: The Looming Crisis." *Issues in Science and Technology*. 3(4):52–63.

Cooper, Jay M., and Robert M. Houck (1983). "Study Protocol, Criteria, and Complications of the Silicone Plug Procedure." In Gerald I. Zatuchni, James D. Shelton, Alfredo Goldsmith, and John J. Sciarra, eds., *Female Transcervical Sterilization*. Philadelphia: Harper and Row. Pp. 255–269.

Council on Environmental Quality (1981). *Chemical Hazards to Human Reproduction*. Washington, D.C.: Government Printing Office.

Council on Scientific Affairs (1982). "Maternal Serum Alpha-Fetoprotein

Monitoring." *Journal of the American Medical Association* 247:1478.

Crane, Diana (1975). *The Sanctity of Social Life: Physicians' Treatment of Critically Ill Patients*. New York: Russell Sage Foundation.

Cross, Peter J., and Barry J. Gurland (1987). "The Epidemiology of Dementing Disorders." Contract report prepared for Office of Technology Assessment, *Losing a Million Minds*. Springfield, Va.: National Technical Information Service.

Cullen, D. J. (1981). "Surgical Intensive Care: Current Perceptions and Problems." *Critical Care Medicine* 9:263.

Cwiek, Mark A. (1984). "Presumed Consent as a Solution to the Organ Shortfall Problem." *Public Law Forum* 4:81–99.

Davis, Angela Y. (1981). *Women, Race and Class*. New York: Random House.

Delgado, Richard (1982). "Organically Induced Behavioral Change in Correctional Institutions." In Michael H. Shapiro, ed., *Biological and Behavioral Technologies and the Law*. New York: Praeger. Pp. 139–180

Department of Health, Education, and Welfare, National Institutes of Health (1979). *Antenatal Diagnosis: Predictors of Hereditary Disease or Congenital Defects*. Washington, D.C.: Government Printing Office.

Detsky, A. S., S. C. Stricker, A. G. Mulley, and G. E. Thibault (1981). "Prognosis, Survival and the Expenditure of Hospital Resources for Patients in an Intensive Care Unit." *New England Journal of Medicine* 305:667–672.

Diamond, E. F. (1977). "The Deformed Child's Right to Life." In Dennis J. Horan and David Mall, eds., *Death, Dying and Euthanasia*. Washington, D.C.: University Press of America. Pp. 127–138.

Drotman, D. Peter (1987). "Now Is the Time to Prevent AIDS." *American Journal of Public Health* 77(2):143.

Dyer, Allen R. (1986). "Patients, Not Costs, Come First." *Hastings Center Report* 16(1):5–7.

Earl of Listowel (1986). "Foreword." In A. B. Downing and Barbara Smoker, eds., *Voluntary Euthanasia: Experts Debate the Right To Die*. London: Peter Owen. P. i.

Eisner, Victor, J. V. Brazie, M. W. Pratt, and A. C. Hexter (1979). "The Risk of Low Birthweight." *American Journal of Public Health* 69:887.

Elias, Sherman, and George J. Annas (1983). "Perspectives on Fetal Surgery." *American Journal of Obstetrics and Gynecology* 145:807–812.

Elias, Sherman, Joe Leigh Simpson, Alice O. Martin, Rudy E. Sabbagha, Albert B. Gerbie, and Louis G. Keith (1985). "Chronic Villus Sampling for First-Trimester Prenatal Diagnois: Northwestern University Program." *American Journal of Obstetrics and Gynecology* 152: 204–213.

Engelhardt, H. Tristram (1984). "Shattuck Lecture—Allocating Scarce Medical Resources and the Viability of Organ Transplantation." *New England Journal of*

Medicine 311(1):66–71.

Equal Employment Opportunity Commission (1980). "Interpretive Guidelines on Employment Discrimination and Reproductive Hazards." *Federal Register,* February: 7514.

Evans, Roger W. (1983). "Health Care Technology and the Inevitability of Resource Allocation and Rationing Decisions: Part II." *Journal of the American Medical Association* 249(6):2208–2219.

Finamore, Eric P. (1982). *"Jefferson v. Griffin Spaulding County Hospital Authority:* Court-Ordered Surgery to Protect the Life of an Unborn Child." *American Journal of Law and Medicine* 9(1):83–101.

Fletcher, John C. (1981). "The Fetus as a Patient: Ethical Issues." *Journal of the American Medical Association* 246(77):772–773.

——— (1983). "Emerging Ethical Issues in Fetal Therapy." In Kare Berg and Knut E. Tranoy, eds., *Research Ethics.* New York: Alan R. Liss. Pp. 293–318.

Fletcher, Joseph F. (1979). *Humanhood.* Buffalo: Prometheus Books.

Forrest, Jacqueline D., and Stanley K. Henshaw (1983). "What U.S. Women Think and Do about Contraception." *Family Planning Perspectives* 15(4): 157–166.

Fost, Norman, and Ronald E. Cranford (1985). "Hospital Ethics Committees: Administrative Aspects." *Journal of the American Medical Association* 253: 2687–2692.

Fox, Daniel M. (1987). "The Cost of AIDS from Conjecture to Research." *AIDS and Public Policy* 2(1):25–27.

Fox, Renee C., and Judith P. Swazey (1978). *The Courage To Fail: A Social View of Transplantation and Dialysis.* Chicago: University of Chicago Press.

Freeman, David M. (1974). *Technology and Society: Issues in Assessment, Conflict and Choice.* Chicago: Rand McNally.

Friedrich, Otto (1984). "One Miracle, Many Doubts." *Time* (December 10):70–77.

Fuchs, Victor R., and Leslie Perreault (1986). "Expenditures for Reproduction-Related Health Care." *Journal of the American Medical Association* 255:76–81.

Furnish, Hannah A. (1980). "Prenatal Exposure to Fetally Toxic Work Environments: The Dilemma of the 1978 Pregnancy Amendment to Title VII of the Civil Rights Act of 1964." *Iowa Law Review* 66:63–129.

Gallup Report (1983). 213(June):11–12.

Gaylin, Willard (1974). "Harvesting the Dead: The Potential for Recycling Human Bodies." *Harper's* (September):23–30.

Gianelli, Diane M. (1987). "Ethics Panel Members Named." *American Medical News* (August 14):10.

Golbus, M. S., W. D. Loughman, C. J. Epstein, G. Halbash, J. D. Stephens, and B. D. Hall (1979). "Prenatal Genetic Diagnosis in 3000 Amniocenteses." *New England Journal of Medicine* 300:157–163.

Gostin, Larry, and William J. Curran (1987). "AIDS Screening, Confidentiality, and the Duty to Warn." *American Journal of Public Health* 77(3):361–365.

Gray, Bernard H., R. A. Cooke, and A. S. Tannenbaum (1978). "Research Involving Human Subjects." *Science* 201:1094.

Greenwald, Robert A., Mary Kay Ryan, and James E. Mulvihill, eds. (1982). *Human Subjects Research: A Handbook for Institutional Review Boards.* New York: Plenum Press.

Grobstein, Clifford (1978). Statement to the Ethics Advisory Board. September 15, meeting transcript. Washington D.C.: National Technical Information Service.

———— (1979). *A Double Image of the Double Helix.* San Francisco: W. H. Freeman.

———— (1981). *From Chance to Purpose: An Appraisal of External Human Fertilization.* Reading, Mass.: Addison-Wesley.

———— (1982). "The Moral Uses of 'Spare' Embryos." *Hastings Center Report* 12(3):5–6.

Grobstein, Clifford, and Michael Flower (1984) "Gene Therapy: Proceed With Caution." *Hastings Center Report* 14(2):13–17.

Hale, Ellen (1984). "Is There Life after Transplant?" *American Health* (January-February):58–62.

Hanft, R. (1977). Testimony before Senate Subcommittee on Health and Scientific Research. In Tabitha M. Powledge and L. Dachs, eds., *Biomedical Research and the Public.* Washington D.C.: Government Printing Office.

Hanson, J. W. (1980). "Reproductive Wastage and Prenatal Ethanol Exposure: Human and Animal Studies." In I. H. Porter and Ernest B. Hook, eds., *Human Embryonic and Fetal Death.* New York: Academic Press. Pp. 221–223.

Hardy, Ann M., Kathryn Rauch, Dean Echenberg, W. Meade Morgan, and James W. Curran (1986). "The Economic Impact of the First 10,000 Cases of Acquired Immunodeficiency Syndrome in the United States." *Journal of the American Medical Association* 255:209–215.

Harris, Jeffrey E. (1987). "The AIDS Epidemic: Looking into the 1990s." *Technology Review* 90(5):58–65.

Harrison, Michael R., Mitchell S. Golbus, and Roy A. Filly (1981). "Management of the Fetus with a Correctable Congenital Defect." *Journal of the American Medical Association* 146(7):774–777.

Harrison, Michael R., Mitchell S. Golbus, Roy A. Filly, Peter W. Callen, Michael Katz, Alfred DeLorimier, Mark Rosen, and Albert Jonsen (1982). "Fetal Surgery for Congenital Hydronephrosis." *New England Journal of Medicine* 306(10):591–593.

Harron, Frank, John Burnside, and Tom Beauchamp (1983). *Health and Human Values.* New Haven: Yale University Press.

Harsanyi, Zsolt, and R. Hutton (1981). *Genetic Prophecy: Beyond the Double Helix.*

New York: Rawson, Wade.

Hartley, S. F., and L. M. Pietracyzk (1979). "Preselecting the Sex of Offspring: Technologies, Attitudes and Implications." *Social Biology* 26(3):232–246.

Henry, Alice, Ward Rinehart, and Phyllis Piotrow (1980). "Reversing Female Sterilization." *Population Reports* (September): C-8.

Hiatt, H. H. (1975). "Protecting the Medical Commons: Who Is Responsible?" *New England Journal of Medicine* 293:235–240.

Hill, J. D., J. R. Hampton, and J. R. A. Mitchell (1978). "A Randomized Trial of Home versus Hospital Management of Patients with Suspected Myocardial Infarction." *The Lancet* 1978(1):837–841.

Holden, Constance (1982). "Looking at Genes in the Workplace." *Science* 217: 336–337.

Horowitz, D. I. (1977). *The Courts and Social Policy.* Washington, D.C.: The Brookings Institute.

Howard, Linda G. (1981). "Hazardous Substances in the Workplace: Rights of Women." *University of Pennsylvania Law Review* 129:798–845.

Hubbard, Ruth, and M. S. Henifin (1985). "Genetic Screening of Prospective Parents and of Workers: Some Scientific and Social Issues." *International Journal of Health Services* 15(2):231–251.

Hughes, A. L. (1981). "Female Infanticide: Sex Ratio Manipulation in Humans." *Ethology and Sociobiology* 2:109–111.

Hummel, Robert F. (1987). "AIDS, Public Policy, and Insurance." *AIDS and Public Policy Journal* 2(1):1.

Humphry, Derek, and Ann Wickett (1986). *The Right To Die: Understanding Euthanasia.* New York: Harper and Row.

Hunt, Vilma R. (1975). *Occupational Health Problems of Pregnant Women.* Washington, D.C.: Department of Health, Education and Welfare.

——— (1978). "Occupational Radiation Exposure of Women Workers." *Preventive Medicine* 7:294–299.

Ingelfinger, Franz J. (1980). "Medicine: Meritorious or Meretricious?" In Philip H. Abelson, ed., *Health Care: Regulation, Economics, Ethics, Practice.* Washington, D.C.: American Association for the Advancement of Science. Pp. 141–145.

Ingraham, B. L., and G. W. Smith (1972). "The Use of Electronics in the Observation and Control of Human Behavior and Its Possible Use in Rehabilitation and Parole." *Issues in Criminology* 7:35–53.

Institute of Medicine (1987). "Confronting AIDS: Directions for Public Health, Health Care, and Research." *Issues in Science and Technology* 3(2):92–101.

Isaacs, Stephen L., and Renee J. Holt (1987). "Redefining Procreation: Facing the Issues." *Population Bulletin* 42(3):1–37.

Jonsen, Albert R. (1986). "The Artificial Heart's Threat to Others." *Hastings Center Report* 16(1):9–11.

Judicial Council of the American Medical Association (1982). *Current Opinion.* Chicago: American Medical Association.

Kass, Leon R. (1976). "Implications of Prenatal Diagnosis for the Human Right to Life." In James M. Humber and Robert F. Almeder, eds., *Biomedical Ethics and the Law.* New York: Plenum Press. Pp. 335350.

———— (1978). "Ethical Issues in Human *In Vitro* Fertilization, Embryo Culture and Research, and Embryo Transfer." Unpublished paper prepared for the Ethics Advisory Board, Department of Health, Education, and Welfare. Washington, D.C.: Government Printing Office. Appendix 2.

Katz, Jay (1972). *Experimentation With Human Beings.* New York: Russell Sage Foundation.

Katz, B. F. (1978). "Legal Implications of In Vitro Fertilization and Its Regulation." Unpublished paper prepared for the Ethics Advisory Board, Department of Health, Education, and Welfare. Washington D.C.: Government Printing Office.

Kerenyi, T. D., and U. Chitkara (1981). "Selective Birth in Twin Pregnancy with Discordancy for Down's Syndrome." *New England Journal of Medicine* 304: 1525–1527.

Kevles, Daniel J. (1985). *In the Name of Eugenics: Genetics and the Use of Human Heredity.* Berkeley: University of California Press.

Kieffer, George H. (1975). *Ethical Issues in the Life Sciences.* New York: American Association for the Advancement of Science.

King, Patricia A. (1980). "The Juridical Status of the Fetus: A Proposal for the Protection of the Unborn." In C. E. Schneider and M. A. Vinovskis, eds., *The Law and Politics of Abortion.* Lexington, Mass.: Lexington Books. Pp. 81–121.

Kirkley, William H. (1980). "Fetal Survival—What Price?" *American Journal of Obstetrics and Gynecology* 137 (August):873.

Knaus, William A. (1986). "Rationing, Justice, and the American Physician." *Journal of the American Medical Association* 255(9):1176–1177.

Kolata, Gina (1986a). "Manic-Depression: Is It Inherited?" *Science* 232 (May 2): 575–576.

———— (1986b). "Genetic Screening Raises Questions for Employers and Insurers." *Science* 232 (April 18):317–319.

———— (1986c). "Researchers Hunt for Alzheimer's Disease Gene." *Science* 232 (April 25):448–450.

———— (1986d). "Researchers Seek Melanoma Gene." *Science* 232 (May 9):708–709.

Lenow, Jeffrey L. (1983). "The Fetus as a Patient: Emerging Rights as a Person?" *American Journal of Law and Medicine* 9(1):1–29.

Lewin, Roger (1987). "National Academy Looks at Human Genome Project, Sees Progress." *Science* 235:747–748.

Lewis, Hilary (1987). "Acquired Immunodeficiency Syndrome: State Legislative Activity." *Journal of the American Medical Association* 258 (17):2410–2414.

Loewy, Erich H. (1980). "Cost Should Not Be a Factor in Medical Care." *New England Journal of Medicine* 302:697.

Lundberg, George D. (1983). "Rationing Human Life." *Journal of the American Medical Association* 249 (16):2223–2224.

Macri, J. N., and R. R. Weiss (1982). "Prenatal Serum Alpha-Fetoprotein Screening for Neural Tube Defects." *Obstetrics and Gynecology* 59(5):633.

Main, Denise M., and Michael T. Mennuti (1986). "Neural Tube Defects: Issues in Prenatal Diagnosis and Counselling." *Obstetrics and Gynecology* 67(1):1–16.

Mark, Vernon H., and Frank R. Ervin (1970). *Violence and the Brain*. New York: Harper and Row.

Matheny, Albert R., and Bruce A. Williams (1981). "Scientific Disputes and Adversary Procedures in Policy Making." *Law and Policy Quarterly* 3(3):341–364.

Mathieu, Deborah (1984). "The Baby Doe Controversy." *Arizona State Law Journal* 1984(4):602–626.

Matthewman, William D. (1984). "Title VII and Genetic Testing: Can Your Genes Screen You Out of a Job?" *Howard Law Journal* 27 (Fall):1185–1224.

Mattson, L. P. (1981). "The Pregnancy Amendment: Fetal Rights and the Workplace." *Case and Comment* (November-December):33–41.

May, Marlynn L. (1981). "Governing Standards of Medical Care." In R. A. L. Gambitta, M. L. May, and J. S. Foster, eds., *Governing Through Courts*. Beverly Hills, Calif.: Sage. Pp. 110–131.

Maynard-Moody, S. (1979). "The Fetal Research Dispute." In Dorothy Nelkin. ed., *Controversy*. Beverly Hills, Calif.: Sage.

Mechanic, David (1977). "The Growth of Medical Technology and Bureaucracy: Implications for Medical Care." *Milbank Memorial Fund Quarterly* 55 (Winter): 61–78.

———— (1981). "Some Dilemmas in Health Care Policy." *Milbank Memorial Fund Quarterly* 59(1):1–15

———— (1986). *From Advocacy to Allocation: The Evolving American Health Care System*. New York: Free Press.

Medical World News (1987). "AIDS Drug Cost Creates New Dilemma." *Medical World News* (April 13):17–18.

Melnick, M. (1980). "Drugs as Etiological Agents in Mental Retardation and other Developmental Anomalies of the Central Nervous System." In Michael K. McCormack, ed., *Prevention of Mental Retardation and Other Developmental Disabilities*. New York: Marcel Dekker.

Miller, C. Arden (1984). "The Health of Children, a Crisis in Ethics." *Pediatrics* 73(4):550–558.

Miller, Francis H., and Graham A. H. Miller (1986). "The Painful Prescription:

A Procrustean Perspective." *New England Journal of Medicine* 314(21):1383–1385.

Mirsky, A. F., and M. H. Orzack (1977). "Final Report on Psychosurgery Pilot Study." In *Appendix: Psychosurgery*. Washington, D.C.: Government Printing Office.

Mulley, Albert G. (1981). "The Allocation of Resources for Medical Intensive Care." In President's Commission for the Study of Ethical Problems in Medicine and Biomedical and Behavorial Research, *Securing Access to Health Care*. Washington, D.C.: Government Printing Office.

Murphy, E. A., G. Chase, and A. Rodriguez (1978). "Genetic Intervention: Some Social, Psychological, and Philosophical Aspects." In B. H. Cohen, A. Lilienfeld, and P. C. Haung, eds., *Genetic Issues in Public Health and Medicine*. Springfield, Ill.: Charles C Thomas. Pp.358–398.

Murray, Thomas H. (1984). "Ethics and Health Care Allocation." *Public Law Forum* 4:41–50.

National Commission for the Protection of Human Subjects (1975). *Research on the Fetus*. Washington, D.C.: Government Printing Office.

National Conference of Commissioners on Uniform State Laws (1987). "Uniform Brain Death Act." *Uniform Laws Annotated* 12:15.

Newhouse, J. P., W. G. Manning, C. N. Morris, L. L. Orr, and N. Dean (1981). "Some Interim Results from a Controlled Trial of Cost Sharing in Health Insurance." *New England Journal of Medicine* 305(25):1501–1507.

Nishimura, H., and T. Tanimura (1976). *Clinical Aspects of the Teratogenicity of Drugs*. Amsterdam: Excerpta Medica.

Office of Health Economics (1979). "Scarce Resources in Health Care." *Milbank Memorial Fund Quarterly* 57(2):371–392.

Office of Medical Applications of Research, National Institutes of Health (1984). "The Use of Diagnostic Ultrasound Imaging during Pregnancy." *Journal of the American Medical Association* 252(5):669–672.

Office of Technology Assessment (1981a). *Impacts of Applied Genetics: Micro-Organisms, Plants, and Animals*. Washington, D.C.: Government Printing Office.

——— (1981b). *The Costs and Effectiveness of Neonatal Intensive Care*. Washington, D.C.: Government Printing Office.

——— (1987a). *OTA Proposal: Infertility Prevention and Treatment*. Washington, D.C.: OTA.

——— (1987b). *Losing a Million Minds: Confronting the Tragedy of Alzheimer's Disease and Other Dementias*. Washington, D.C.: Government Printing Office.

Olson, Steve (1986). *Biotechnology: An Industry Comes of Age*. Washington, D.C.: National Academy Press.

Partington, M. W. (1986). "X-Linked Mental Retardation: Caveats in Genetic Counseling." *American Journal of Medical Genetics* 23(1–2):101–109.

Pellegrino, Edmund D. (1986). "Rationing Health Care: The Ethics of Medical Gatekeeping." *Journal of Contemporary Health Law and Policy* 2:23–46.

Perry, Tracy B. (1985). "Fetoscopy." *Progress in Clinical and Biological Research* 163B:207–212.

Petchesky, Rosalind P. (1979). "Reproduction, Ethics, and Public Policy: The Federal Sterilization Regulations." *Hastings Center Report* 9 (October):29–41.

Philip, J., and J. Bang (1985). "Prenatal Diagnosis in Multiple Gestations." In Karen Filkins and Joseph F. Russo, eds., *Human Prenatal Diagnosis*. New York: Marcel Dekker. Pp. 169–182.

Pinkney, Deborah S. (1987). "Manpower Crisis: Growing Labor Shortage in all Areas Crippling Hospitals across Nation." *American Medical News* (November 20):1, 12.

Poe, M. (1981). "Health Law: Preservation of Life—A Right To Be Born." *American Journal of Trial Advocacy* 5 (Fall):383–388.

President's Commission for the Study of Ethical Problems in Medicine and Biomedical and Behavioral Research (1981). *Defining Death*. Washington, D.C.: Government Printing Office.

——— (1983a). *Deciding to Forego Life-Sustaining Treatment*. Washington, D.C.: Government Printing Office.

——— (1983). *Securing Access to Health Care*. Washington, D.C.: Government Printing Office.

Purdy, L. M. (1978). "Genetic Diseases: Can Having Children Be Immoral?" In J. J. Buckley, ed., *Genetics Now: Ethical Issues in Genetic Research*. Washington, D.C.: University Press of America.

Quinlan, R. William, Amelia C. Cruz, and John F. Huddleston (1986). "Sonographic Detection of Urinary-Tract Anomalies." *Obstetrics and Gynecology* 67(2):558–570.

Quist, Norman (1987). "AIDS and Public Policy: Publisher's Introduction." *AIDS and Public Policy Journal* 1(1):1–2.

Ramsey, Paul (1970). *Fabricated Man: The Ethics of Genetic Control*. New Haven, Conn.: Yale University Press.

——— (1975). *The Ethics of Fetal Research*. New Haven, Conn.: Yale University Press.

Rawls, R. L. (1980). "Reproductive Hazards in the Workplace." *Chemical and Engineering News* (February):28–30.

Reilly, Philip (1977). *Genetics, Law and Social Policy*. Cambridge, Mass.: Harvard University Press.

Reiser, Stanley J. (1985). "Responsibility for Personal Health: A Historical Perspective." *The Journal of Medicine and Philosophy* 10:7–17.

Rhoden, Nancy K., and John D. Arras (1985). "Withholding Treatment from Baby Doe: From Discrimination to Child Abuse." *Milbank Memorial Fund Quarterly*

63(1):18–51.

Ricardo-Campbell, Rita (1980). *The Economics and Politics of Health Care.* Chapel Hill: University of North Carolina Press.

Rist, Ray C., and Ronald J. Anson, eds. (1977). *Education, Social Science, and Judicial Process.* New York: Teachers College Press.

Robertson, John A. (1983a). "Procreative Liberty and the Control of Conception, Pregnancy, and Childbirth." *Virginia Law Review* 69(3):405–464.

——— (1983b) "Medicolegal Implications of a Human Life Amendment." In A. Edward Doudera and Margery W. Shaw, eds., *Defining Human Life.* Ann Arbor, Mich.: Health Administration Press.

Rodgers, Joann Ellison (1984). "Liver Politics: Cruel Decisions." *American Health* (January–February): 62–63.

Rodriguez, Helen (1980). "Concluding Remarks: Depo-Provera and Sterilization Abuse." In Helen B. Holmes, Betty B. Hoskins, and Michael Gross, eds., *Birth Control and Controlling Birth: Women-Centered Perspectives.* Clifton, N.J.: Humana Press. Pp. 125–128.

Rogers, Harrison L., Jr. (1986). "Resisting Pressure." *American Medical News* (June 27–July 4):4.

Rom, William N. (1980). "Effects of Lead on Reproduction." In Peter F. Infante and Marvin S. Legator, eds., *Proceedings of a Workshop on Methodology for Assessing Reproductive Hazards in the Workplace.* Washington, D.C.: National Institute for Occupational Safety and Health. Pp. 33–42.

Rosen, Paul L. (1972). *The Supreme Court and Social Science.* Urbana: University of Illinois Press.

Rosenfeld, Albert (1982). "The Patient in the Womb." *Science* 82:18–23.

Ruddick, W., and W. Wilcox. (1982) "Operating on the Fetus." *Hastings Center Report* 12(5):10–14.

Russell, Louise B. (1986). *Is Prevention Better Than Cure?* Washington, D.C.: The Brookings Institution.

Saward, Ernest, and Andrew Sorensen (1980). "The Current Emphasis on Preventive Medicine." In Philip H. Abelson, ed., *Health Care: Regulation, Economics, Ethics, Practice.* Washington, D.C.: American Association for the Advancement of Science. Pp. 49–54.

Schechner, Sylvia (1980). "For the 1980s: How Small Is Too Small?" *Clinics in Perinatology* 7 (March):142.

Scherzer, Mark (1987). "AIDS and Insurance: The Case against HIV Antibody Testing." *AIDS and Public Policy Journal* 2(1):19–24.

Schramm, Carl J. (1984). "Can We Solve the Hospital-Cost Problem in Our Democracy?" *New England Journal of Medicine* 311(11):729–732.

Schroeder, John Speer, and Sharon Hunt (1987). "Cardiac Transplantation." *Journal of the American Medical Association* 258 (21):3142–3145.

Schuck, Peter H. (1981). "Malpractice Liability and the Rationing of Care." *Texas Law Review* 59:1421–1425.

Scitovsky, Anne A., and Dorothy P. Rice (1987). "Estimates of the Direct and Indirect Costs of Acquired Immunodeficiency Syndrome in the United States, 1985, 1986, and 1991." *Public Health Reports* 102(1):5–17.

Scriver, Charles R., (1985). "Population Screening: Report of a Workshop." *Progress in Clinical and Biological Research* 163B:89–152.

Sewell, Sandra S. (1980). "Sterilization Abuse and Hispanic Women." In Helen B. Holmes, Betty B. Hoskins, and Michael Gross, eds., *Birth Control and Controlling Birth: Women-Centered Perspectives.* Clifton, N. J.: Humana Press. Pp. 121–123.

Shapiro, Donald L., and Paul Rosenberg (1984). "The Effect of Federal Regulations regarding Handicapped Newborns." *Journal of the American Medical Association* 252:2031–2033.

Shapiro, Michael H. (1982). "Legislating the Control of Behavior Control." In Michael H. Shapiro, ed., *Biological and Behavioral Technologies and the Law.* New York: Praeger. Pp. 49–138.

Shapiro, Sam M., M. C. McCormick, B. H. Starfield, J. P. Krisher, and D. Boss (1980). "Relevance of Correlates of Infant Deaths for Significant Morbidity at One Year of Age." *American Journal of Obstetrics and Gynecology* 136(3):363–366.

Shick, Alan (1977). "Complex Policy Making in the United States Senate." In *Policy Analyses on Major Issues prepared for the Commission on the Operation of the Senate.* Washington, D.C.: Government Printing Office. Pp. 1–26.

Short, R. V. (1978). "Human In Vitro Fertilization and Embryo Transfer." Unpublished paper prepared for the Ethics Advisory Board, Department of Health, Education, and Welfare. Washington, D.C.: Government Printing Office.

Siegler, Mark (1986). "Ethics Committees: Decisions by Bureaucracy." *Hastings Center Report* 16 (June):22–24.

Simpson, Joe Leigh (1986). "Methods for Detecting Neural Tube Defects." *Contemporary OB/GYN* 1986:202–222.

Singer, Eleanor, and Theresa F. Rogers (1986). "Public Opinion and AIDS." *AIDS and Public Policy Journal* 1(1):8–13.

Smith, J. M. (1977). "Congenital Minimata Disease: Methyl Mercury Poisoning and Birth Defects in Japan." In Eula Bingham, ed., *Proceedings: Conference on Women and the Workplace.* Washington, D.C.: Society for Occupational and Environmental Health.

Society for the Right To Die (1987). *Handbook of Living Will Laws.* New York: Society for the Right To Die.

Strauss, Michael J., J. P. LoGerfo, J. A. Yeltatzie, N. Temkin, and L. D. Hudson (1986). "Rationing of Intensive Care Unit Services: An Everyday Occurrence." *Journal of the American Medical Association* 255(9):1143–1146.

Strom, Terry B., and Rolf Loertscher (1984). "Cyclosporine-Induced Nephrotoxicity: Inevitable and Intractable." *New England Journal of Medicine* 311(11): 728–729.

Strong, Carson (1983). "The Tiniest Newborns." *Hastings Center Report* 13(5):14–19.

Szasz, Thomas (1974). *The Myth of Mental Illness,* rev. ed. New York: Harper and Row.

Teuber, H. L., S. H. Corkin, and T. E. Twitchell (1977). "Study of Cingulotomy in Man: A Summary." In W. H. Sweet, S. Obrador, and J. G. Martin-Rodriquez, eds., *Neurosurgical Treatment in Psychiatry, Pain, and Epilepsy.* Baltimore, Md.: University Park Press. Pp. 355–362.

Thurow, Lester C. (1985). "Medicine versus Economics." *New England Journal of Medicine* 313(10):611–614.

Valenstein, Elliot S., ed. (1980). *The Psychosurgery Debate: Scientific, Legal, and Ethical Perspectives.* San Francisco, Calif.: W. H. Freeman Company.

———— (1986). *Great and Desperate Cures: The Rise and Decline of Psychosurgery and Other Radical Treatments for Mental Illness.* New York: Basic Books.

Valentine, Jeannette M., and Alonzo L. Plough (1983). "Protecting the Reproductive Health of Workers: Problems in Science and Public Policy." *Journal of Health Politics, Policy, and Law* 8(1):144–163.

Verp, Marion S., and Joe Leigh Simpson (1985). "Amniocentesis for Cytogenetic Studies." In Karen Filkins and Joesph F. Russo, eds., *Human Prenatal Diagnosis.* New York: Marcel Dekker. Pp. 13–41.

Walters, Leroy (1975). "Ethical and Public Policy Issues in Fetal Research." In National Commission for the Protection of Human Subjects, *Research on the Fetus.* Washington, D.C.: Government Printing Office. Pp. 8-1 to 8-12.

Wardle, L. D. (1980). *The Abortion Privacy Doctrine: A Compendium and Critique of Court Abortion Cases.* Buffalo: William S. Heim and Company.

Warsof, Steven L., Derek J. Cooper, David Little, and Stuart Campbell (1986). "Routine Ultrasound Screening for Antenatal Detection of Intrauterine Growth Retardation." *Obstetrics and Gynecology* 67(1):33–38.

Wehr, Elizabeth (1984). "National Health Policy Sought for Organ Transplant Surgery." *Congressional Quarterly Weekly Report* (February 25):453–458.

Willett, Walter C., and Brian MacMahon (1984). "Diet and Cancer—An Overview." *New England Journal of Medicine* 310(10):633–638.

Williams, P., and G. Stevens (1982). "What Now for Test Tube Babies?" *New Scientist* 93(129):312–317.

Williams, Wendy W. (1981). "Firing the Woman to Protect the Fetus: The Reconciliation of Fetal Protection with Employment Opportunity Goals Under Title VII." *Georgetown Law Journal* 69:641–704.

Wimberley, Edward T. (1982). "The RSP Method of Tubal Occlusion: A Review and Update." *Biomedical Bulletin* 3(1):1–6.

Yellin, Joel (1981). "High Technology and the Courts: Nuclear Power and the Need for Institutional Reform." *Harvard Law Review* 94(3):489–560.

Young, Ernle W. D. (1983). "Caring for Disabled Infants." *Hastings Center Report* 13(8):15–18.

Youngblood, J. Craig, and Parker C. Folse III (1981). "Can Courts Govern? An Inquiry into Capacity and Purpose." In R. A. L. Gambitta, M. L. May, and J. Foster, eds., *Governing through Courts*. Beverly Hills, Calif.: Sage. Pp. 23–65.

Youngner, Stuart J. (1987). "DNR Orders: No Longer Secret, But Still a Problem." *Hastings Center Report* 17(1):24–33.

Index